Arts Camp

Christina Clark

Morehouse Publishing
NEW YORK

Morehouse Publishing, 19 East 34th Street, New York, NY 10016

Morehouse Publishing is an imprint of Church Publishing Incorporated.

www.churchpublishing.org

Cover design: Laurie Westhafer

Interior design and production: Helen H. Harrison

Library of Congress Cataloging-in-Publication Data
A catalog record of this book is available from the Library of Congress

ISBN 13: 978-0-8192-3228-1 (pbk)

ISBN 13: 978-0-8192-3229-8 (ebook)

Printed in the United States of America

To Jane Schmitz, who created Arts Camp.

To the Rev. Deb Angell, Mary Ellen Garrett, Linda Frederick, David Bell, and Gene George, who make Arts Camp the best week of the year every summer.

To Karen, Ben, and Jacob who are my universe.

And to the entire St. Barnabas Parish Community for their constant love and support of our children and youth.

All this we do in the name of God: Creator, Redeemer, and Sustainer.

TABLE OF CONTENTS

Introduction

ONE SUNDAY EACH SUMMER, FAMILIES GATHER at St. Barnabas Episcopal Church in Denver, CO for the 9:30 a.m. service to listen to and look at the creations of proud Campers. Nothing beats the radiant face and sparkling eyes of a child as s/he performs a favorite camp song or urges parents to come see her/his work. This celebration has happened every summer since 2001.

How did this tradition begin?

In 2001 my pastor, The Reverend Georgia Humphrey, hired me to create a Family Ministry Program. I began by interviewing the kids and adults who were enrolled at St. Barnabas. The answers they gave helped me design a program for all children and their parents. Our Campers came from all over the Denver Metro area. Building a community of kids and adults was a top priority. We wanted the kids and their parents to know that St. Barnabas welcomed them and was *their church*. It seemed that a summer event might "feed" the sense of community. What kind of event could we offer? I thought about a Vacation Bible School (VBS) program like the ones I'd run in other church settings, but traditional VBS attendance in other churches was diminishing. In addition, we needed something that might attract kids who didn't attend St. Barnabas.

I decided to create a Music Camp, which would involve Bible Stories, crafts, cooperative games, movement, and singing. Kids wouldn't need to have any prior musical experience. Camp would have a theme based on biblical stories or passages that involved music and would be structured in such a way that Campers as well as volunteers would have fun. Would the kids and their families respond to this idea? Only time would tell.

In June of 2001 the first Music Camp began. A posted schedule let everyone see what was planned for each part of the day. Quality volunteers were recruited. Musicians were offered a small stipend to work with the kids. At the end of camp, students filled out an evaluation. On the Sunday immediately following the camp, Campers shared some of what they'd experienced. The congregation loved it. Kids and parents loved it. Success!

During and after camp, volunteers and I reviewed each session to reflect on what worked and what didn't. For instance, we discovered that camp worked best for kids who had just completed first grade through kids who had just completed fifth grade. Kindergarteners didn't have enough stamina for the intensity of our daily schedule, and sixth graders didn't like being at camp with "babies." Providing lunch worked better than having kids bring lunches. Each year we used information from the previous year to make camp better.

Music Camp continued successfully from 2001–2005. Over the years kids had varied experiences: vocal choirs, bell choir, drums, rhythm sticks, movement to music, dances of universal peace, and rhythm instruments. We made drums, rain sticks, ocean drums, rhythm instruments, etc. We presented Bible stories through skits, songs, scripts, storytelling, and more.

However, I began to get feedback from the kids indicating a feeling of "been there, done that." Once again using participant feedback, I decided that an Arts Camp would give us multiple ways to develop the summer program. We would use the same organizational pieces in Arts Camp that we successfully employed for Music Camp. Again, biblical themes and stories were the basis for the camp.

The first Arts Camp happened in 2006. Three artists—a sculptor, an artist who taught acrylic painting, and a dramatic reading coach—helped us change the focus of our week of camp and generate enthusiasm. The Sunday service after the close of camp remained one of the best ways to share each year's camp experience.

All of these Music and Arts Camp experiences brought great joy to my life. Working with a team of volunteers and artists proved to be an avenue of spiritual growth for students as well as the rest of us.

The last Camp I conducted was in the summer of 2009. I retired in January of 2010. Tina Clark is now the Family Minister at St. Barnabas. Tina and I collaborated for many years. She was an outstanding and committed volunteer. From 2010 to the present, she has continued to provide camps that bring joy and understanding to St. Barnabas's children and children from the surrounding community. As a former grade-school teacher, Tina knows about education. Possessing a highly inventive mind and spiritual depth, Tina Clark is eminently qualified to write about the process of creating and operating an Arts Camp. Anyone with a similar program or planning to start one will benefit from the expertise and advice presented in this book.

May God continue to bless her ministry . . . and yours as well.

> Peace,
>
> Jane Schmitz, November 2014
> Family Minister
> St. Barnabas Episcopal Church, 2001–2010

PART ONE

HOW TO CREATE ARTS CAMP

CHAPTER 1

What Is Arts Camp?

ARTS CAMP WAS DEVELOPED AS AN ALTERNAtive to pre-packaged Vacation Bible School curriculums by leaders and volunteers at St. Barnabas Episcopal Church in Denver, CO. It began as Music Camp, and expanded to Arts Camp nine years ago. Now in its fifteenth year, this Camp has grown and evolved as a vital and beloved component of our Family Ministry. Kids who attended as our first Campers now help run camp as Senior Counselors, and a new generation of elementary-aged Campers excitedly fill our parish halls and sanctuary with voices, song, and laughter for a week every summer.

Arts Camp uses music and song, visual art and media, drama and storytelling, and movement and game-playing to enter into Bible study around an established theme. Themes have included *Praise, EcoJustice, The Call to Love our Neighbor, Interfaith Spirituality,* and *Saints and Holy Helpers.*

This book offers the basics for creating your own version of Arts Camp, as well as chapters on the specifics for building each of the five themed camps mentioned above. You will find resources, music suggestions, art projects, and sample schedules to help you create a camp that fits your parish's needs, population, theology, and more.

Arts Camp builds community and involves children and youth in active, energetic, scripture-based worship. Arts Camp at St. Barnabas nearly always rotates around a central theology of living into Christ's call to love one

another and to seek peace. All parish children are invited, of course. We also invite and include children from the neighborhood (we are mainly a commuter parish), friends and relatives of parishioners, and children from a local shelter. Through grants and careful stewardship of camp fees, we've offered scholarships to homeless, at-risk, and refugee children.

At St. Barnabas, Arts Camp takes place for a week each summer. The camp runs Monday through Friday, from 9:00 a.m. to 3:00 p.m., with a culminating offering and celebration at that Sunday's worship service. Because of the absolute flexibility that comes with designing your own camp, Arts Camp could be offered in addition to VBS, as a Spring Break option for working parents, as an afterschool program, as a longer half-day camp, or as a Lenten or other seasonal study. A camp that fits your parish's personality, volunteer base, and needs can be adapted in a variety of ways. Beautiful!

We established Arts Camp as an offering for rising first through fifth graders, with middle-school youth participating as Junior Counselors and high-school youth as Senior Counselors. Junior Counselors are full participants in camp, with a discounted camp fee in return for a pledge that they will act as role models and mentors to the younger Campers. Senior Counselors pay only to cover their food and T-shirts (more on that later) and act as assistants to the adults who lead the camp. In general, we hire youth who are active participants in our parish youth group; we know their strengths and can place a high level of trust and responsibility in them.

Note: Throughout the rest of this book, when we speak of "Campers," we include the Junior Counselors, since their overall camp experience is the same as other Campers.

WHY CREATE ARTS CAMP WHEN WE CAN PURCHASE A VBS CURRICULUM?

Perhaps you're ready to try something new and different. Perhaps you're tired of the slickness and superficiality of many pre-packaged VBS programs. Perhaps you've felt that VBS doesn't connect with some of your children the way you'd like to.

Among the reasons we do Arts Camp in place of VBS is that it feels more organic for our parish. Its natural flexibility allows us to shape our structure and content to fit our parish personality and theology, as well as current events or ministries of the parish. We plan scripture and Bible study to support the goals of camp, as well as bring stories and quotes from a variety of non-biblical sources. This level of flexibility also allows us to change the pace and volume of programming each day of camp as needed. Nothing is scripted; you have a list of scripture readings, quotes, and ideas that are ready to use as they fit the direction the kids themselves take you.

Arts Camp Sunday is an energetic and celebratory worship service that has become a parish favorite. It is the culmination of the weeklong camp, and the time when the Campers offer what they've done, learned, discovered, explored, and created within our theme. Every year, there is a place in the service when the entire camp steps up and presents to the congregation. We refer to this presentation as the "Arts Camp Offering." Additionally, the entire service includes hymns and readings that have been meaningful during our weeklong camp. In 2013, following our Interfaith Camp Offering, a parishioner who is vocally not fond of children leading worship shared with us how much he'd learned from and enjoyed what the Campers brought to the Arts Camp Sunday service.

Throughout this book, the part of the service wherein Arts Camp takes the leadership role is referred to as the Arts Camp Offering. The service itself is Arts Camp Sunday. While the Offering can also be referred to as "sharing" or a "presentation," it is never called a performance, as it is never our goal to put children on the altar as entertainment, but to be an integral and vital part of our corporate worship.

Because of the organic and flexible nature of a camp you create yourself, the Sunday Offering evolves as a product of the kids' energy, interests, and leadership each year. Each specific themed camp chapter will tell you more about how to develop an Arts Camp Sunday Offering, and how to work with clergy to plan the whole of your Arts Camp Sunday service.

Lastly, by creating our own theme and camp, we are able to offer a faith-based camp that focuses on social justice and compassion. Our goal each year is to remind kids that they are the peacemakers of their generation and that they have the potential to create a lasting peace through active, compassionate living. This is the goal that fits for us. With a camp you create yourself, you can likewise direct your focus to fit that of your parish community's life in Christ.

HOW DO WE PLAN AN ARTS CAMP?

Building your camp from the ground up may sound daunting, but any parish of any size can do it. You will need to create a team with a set of talents—administration, program development, visual art, music, drama and movement, and support—and they may be closer than you think.

Camp Director:

This is most likely you—the Children's Minister or Faith Formation Leader who is reading this resource. This person takes on the organization, planning, leadership, administration, and day-to-day running of Arts Camp. At St. Barnabas, this person also does the Bible study and program aspects of camp. For your camp, especially if it is a larger camp of 50 or more Campers, it may work better to have other Adult Volunteers who run Bible Study and Programming, leaving the Director free to manage the overall camp.

Parishioners:

Look within your own congregation. Do you have any art, music, or drama teachers who worship with you every week? Many teachers are off during the summer and would love to make a small stipend while sharing their skill with the children of your parish. They may also welcome the opportunity to combine their spiritual life with their teaching talents, which they cannot do if they teach in a public school system.

At St. Barnabas we're immensely blessed: our entire Arts Camp team currently comes from within our parish. Our Art Instructors are visual artists and local art teachers who have time and talent they enjoy sharing with our kids. Our parish's choir director happens to be a gifted composer and music teacher with myriad gifts to offer our Campers, while our Associate Rector brings music, accompaniment, and her own scriptural knowledge and input to our sessions. Finally we have a wonderfully creative musician and storyteller who offers movement and song as well as stories, dramatic play, and accompaniment on the hammered dulcimer. In the past, we've had theater and drama teachers as well. Right now, movement and dramatic play fit our Campers best.

Local Artists:

If the art or music teachers in your congregation are travelling or simply looking forward to being away from kids this summer, chances are good that they or other parishioners know someone who would be interested. Does a parishioner have a grown child or niece or nephew who teaches art and could use a little extra money? Does your city or town have a gallery district, art museum, or artists' cooperative where you might advertise? Artists are all around us. Many of them have time and

talent to share and would welcome a small extra pay-check next summer. A piano teacher, school band or orchestra leader, or community theater actor or actress may be available.

One note about hiring artists: not all talented artists are also skilled teachers. Interview these folks carefully, ask about teaching experience and references, and invite them to a Sunday School class to share their skills with the kids. If they have brilliant ideas for projects but cannot communicate effectively with children or demonstrate how to implement these brilliant ideas, everyone will be frustrated during camp.

Do It Yourself:

Maybe you have the creative gene and can lead art projects yourself. If that's the case, go for it, but make sure you plan your time and transitions carefully. If you're leading art, then are also in charge of the next part of the schedule, you will need dependable Adult Volunteers and Counselors to help with cleaning up and wrangling stragglers.

In the first decade of Arts Camp, Art Instructors changed from year to year, while in the last few years we've been able to build and keep a team that works together well, enjoys the time with each other and with the children, and creates an increasingly seamless experience each year. Neither system is preferable in and of itself; what matters most is creating a team that works for your camp.

Adult Volunteers:

Adult Volunteers are a great resource. Look for people to travel from one activity to the next with the Campers, to model desirable behavior, to help a little one who's struggling for any reason, and to report any hiccups to you. These folks are invaluable and should never be turned away! One year a camp parent sent her children's nanny to camp with them and she was worth her weight in gold!

We also recruit two or three Adult Volunteers for each day's lunchtime. These people come in to set out a buffet for the children, monitor and restock as necessary during lunch, and then clean up while the Campers and Leaders head into our afternoon together. It is easy duty, and many parishioners who love to help but lack the time, desire, energy, or talent for working directly with kids sign up year after year. Ask these people to arrive about 30 minutes before you want to serve lunch, and to plan on being there until about 15 minutes after lunchtime ends. A checklist of instructions for them is included with other forms in Appendix 2 (p. 115).

It also works well to split the Campers into two smaller groups to work with one adult at a time; so while one group of about 15 is with our Music Instructor learning or writing songs, the other same-size group is enjoying their storytelling, movement, and dramatic playtime. They switch halfway through the session so all Campers have the same activities by the end of the day. Counselors are assigned to each group and are an essential resource.

Please remember to follow the procedures and policies of your church's governing body in terms of training and safety procedures whenever you use volunteers. In The Episcopal Church, all adults who work at camp must have an active certificate in Safeguarding God's Children; a course that can be taken in person or online. Many parishes also hold an in-person Safeguarding training for youth volunteers.

Building Use and Spatial Considerations:

We use separate parts of our building for almost every component of the Arts Camp day, which makes transitions go smoothly. At the minimum, you need these spaces:

- *An open space where everyone can sit together in a circle.* We have a movable wall that we use to create a slightly smaller space in our large parish hall. We also hang posters of scripture passages and quotations on this wall as we use them for programming. Because we use this same space to set out our lunch buffet, for our meditation and yoga after lunch, and for movement and drama in the afternoon, we need it uncluttered. We keep the space organized by providing several large, round plastic bins for the Campers' personal items, a bookshelf and box for supplies, and a rolling cart for a five-gallon water jug and the Campers' water bottles.

- *A large space for the "Art Room."* You want room for several tables, some to hold supplies and materials, and the rest for kids to have plenty of space to work on their projects. It is certainly best if you can arrange for no other use of this room for the week, so projects and materials can be left out at the end of each day. If that's not possible, make sure you and your Art Instructor plan for time, space, and volunteers to clear out the room and store projects and supplies at the end of the day's Art session(s).

- *Separate spaces for music and movement/drama.* We use the sanctuary for our music room. It is a lovely, light-filled space in the afternoons, and on hot days has the benefit of a swamp cooler—the rest of our 130-year-old building relies on portable fans and air conditioners. It also offers a piano. For movement and drama, we return to the large, open, circle space used in the mornings. Because we keep this space uncluttered, it supports nicely whatever our Drama and Movement Instructor has planned for the day, with lots of area for kids to dance, jump, role-play, and more.

CHAPTER 2

We've Built an Arts Camp Team...
Now What?

THIS CHAPTER GIVES YOU A PLANNING TIMELINE to follow once you've recruited the artists you need to make camp happen.

FIVE TO SIX MONTHS BEFORE CAMP

Date:

Set a date for your camp. Work with clergy, your artistic team, and other scheduled parish events to find a date that works for everyone; remember to include Arts Camp Sunday immediately following camp week. Setting a date and announcing it in January helps parents plan. This is important, since other summer camps usually begin registration in February.

Building Usage:

This is also the time to check with your parish administrator about building use and reserve the spaces you need for the week of camp. Consider reserving the evenings as well, as it is extremely helpful not to have to put everything away at the end of each day. We have two or three groups who graciously cancel their use of our building for Arts Camp, as long as we give them enough notice. And on the Thursday afternoon of our camp, we clean up our large open space extra carefully as it is used as a women's overnight shelter on that day every week. The Campers enjoy knowing that the love, joy, music, prayer, and enthusiasm they leave behind is present for

the women who will be sheltered in that same space that night.

Theme:

Decide on a theme for Arts Camp. There are five to choose from, one each in Chapters 7–11, or perhaps you already have one in mind. For marketing and program purposes, choose a theme that can be described in one word or a short phrase. Keep the theme broad enough that you and your team won't be overly limited in projects, music, scripture, and stories, but specific enough to give everyone a path to follow.

Finances:

You need to establish a fee or cost for camp. Begin by researching weeklong day camps in your area and looking at the average fees for those camps. Also explore what's included for those fees. At St. Barnabas, Arts Camp currently costs $125 for the week, which includes all materials and instruction, lunch and a snack daily, and a T-shirt. (2014 was the first time we increased the camp cost in many years, from $100 to $125, mostly due to higher food prices.) The Junior Counselor fee is $100, and Senior Counselors pay $25 to cover their food and T-shirt (this is probably a little less than the actual cost, but their contribution to the smooth running of camp makes it a bargain). In Denver, this price is well below the average for a five-day summer camp; in your area it may be higher and you should adjust accordingly.

We design Arts Camp to be financially self-sustaining each year. Camp fees are spent on stipends for artists, food, materials, and T-shirts (with a logo) for every participant. Lunch consists of a sandwich bar, with chips, fruit, a vegetable, a dessert, and lemonade, and we order pizza on the Friday. We also provide a Popsicle in the afternoon, and we keep snacks on hand for times when the kids are simply hungry. We ask parents to send a reusable water bottle for the week.

Our camp has evolved to the point where we can charge the above price knowing that most of our families can and will pay it. We've built a scholarship fund over the years, using grants, donations, and careful stewardship of any money we don't spend. We make these funds available to any family based on need. Except for sheltered and refugee families, we generally ask parents to pay at least $25 to $50 if they can. We also offer discounts to families with several children attending camp.

THREE TO FIVE MONTHS BEFORE CAMP

Registration:

Create a flyer—or ask your Art Instructor to do so—and hang it in the parish and the neighborhood. Make announcements to the congregation reminding them that grandchildren, nieces, nephews, cousins, and neighbors' kids who don't normally attend your parish are welcome. Encourage children in your programs to bring a friend from school or the neighborhood. We generally advertise that camp is "gently faith-based with a focus on peace and social justice" to encourage families who might otherwise balk at the idea of a church-sponsored camp.

Our Art Instructor creates a logo or graphic for camp every year, which we use for our flyer and also have printed onto white T-shirts. (We also tie-dye the shirts as one of our art projects.) If you don't already know of a printer in your area who can print these shirts, now is the time to start looking for one. We usually spend no more than $7 per shirt, including the printing, and often keep that closer to $5. We give T-shirts to all Campers, Counselors, Instructors, and Adult Volunteers, and we all wear our finished shirts for the Sunday Offering. We also tie-dyed stoles for our clergy a few years ago, which they wear every year for the service.

There are sample registration forms included in Appendix 2 (pp. 102, 104, and 106) for Campers, Junior Counselors, and Senior Counselors. Your purchase of this book gives you license to adapt and use these materials as needed.

A *Camper's Pledge, Counselor's Pledge,* and *Photo Release* are included in the registration materials. I strongly encourage you to use these or something like them. Giving children and youth an opportunity to buy into their camp registration sends the message that they have an important role in the life of the camp. And in this age of social media and all things digital, we must respect parents' rights to control all of the electronic ways their children's photos end up "out there." Likewise, Counselors must understand that they are never to post a child or youth's photo to any social media or website.

Deposit:

Set a due date for the registration packet and ask for a deposit due at the same time. Registrations should be due to you about two months before camp begins, so that you can plan with your team knowing approximate numbers and ages of Campers and Counselors. We always have late registrations, but at least we know who most of our Campers are before we begin planning.

On Parish and Camp Size:

We are a midsize parish with an average weekly attendance of 100–125. Our annual goal for Camper and Junior Counselor registration is about 24–28, with an additional two to five Senior Counselors. Arts Camp can work, using the guidelines and resources in this book, with a camp as small as 8–10 Campers and only one or two Counselors. For even a very small group, you could certainly run camp with one or two energetic and artistic adults, but it's best to have at least three or four adults; if possible you want the talent and experience of artists and instructors for each camp component. It can also work with a larger group for a larger parish, as long as your parish has the space and Adult Volunteers to accommodate. Regardless of the size of your parish and your camp, strive to have at least one adult leader and one to two Counselors per 12–15 Campers. For a group larger than about 24–30 combined Campers and Counselors, you might also consider cycling through Art, Music, and Movement/Drama throughout the camp day so that each session has a number that remains manageable for your artist Instructors, Counselors, and Adult Volunteers. If you've not done a large camp in the past, it may be best to cap your first year at 24–30 combined Campers and Counselors and build as your resources allow the following year.

Brainstorming Meeting:

At least two months before camp, set up a meeting time for the entire Arts Camp team. Give them the theme ahead of time, as well as an idea of how many and what age Campers are registered. Let them know how long they will be spending with the Campers each day. Ask them to come to the meeting with ideas to share for all aspects of camp. Plan for this meeting to go as long as two hours, and bring as many ideas and suggestions for all aspects of camp as you can: music, songs, art projects, scripture references, and outside resources included.

Have a printed schedule available for each member of your team.

After several years' worth of tweaking, this is a template for the camp schedule that has worked best and run most smoothly at St. Barnabas:

	MONDAY	TUESDAY	WEDNESDAY	THURSDAY	FRIDAY
9:00–9:45	Gather and Morning Program	Gather and Morning Program	Gather and Morning Program	Gather and Morning Program	Gather and Morning Program
9:45–11:15	Art	Art	Art	Art	Art
11:15–11:35	Story and Grace	Story and Grace	Story and Grace	Story and Grace	Story and Grace
11:35–12:15	Lunch and Playtime	Lunch and Playtime	Lunch and Playtime	Lunch and Playtime	Lunch and Playtime
12:15–12:30	Meditation/Yoga	Meditation/Yoga	Meditation/Yoga	Meditation/Yoga	Meditation/Yoga
12:30–2:00	Music and Movement/Drama	Music and Movement/Drama	Music and Movement/Drama	Music and Movement/Drama	Prep for Sunday Offering
2:00–3:00	Popsicles Games Closing	Popsicles Games Closing	Popsicles Games Closing	Popsicles Games Closing	Popsicles Games Closing

Decide how each part of the day is to be handled. For instance, are art projects to be done as a large group in a large space? Will the camp divide for smaller groups for Music and Movement/Drama? Again, if you're a small to midsize parish and camp will have fewer than 30 children, staying together for Art while dividing into two groups for Music and Movement/Drama works well. For a camp larger than 30, dividing into smaller groups and cycling through Art, Music, and Movement/Drama will give Campers and Instructors alike a more relaxed and fulfilling experience. An adapted schedule suggestion for Art, Music, and Movement/Drama with a camp larger than 30 can be found in the section titled "Create Groups" below.

You've taken time to create this team; trust them. Build on each other's ideas, and be open to ideas you may not have considered before. By the end of this meeting, all members of the team should know their responsibilities for both planning and executing the specific camp component that is their realm. They should plan to work together further in smaller teams, at least via email, between now and camp to finalize details. If you have a smaller camp needing one instructor for each part of the day, there will be less need for collaboration, but you still want to make sure each team member knows what the others are planning. For larger parishes, if you have two or more Instructors for any part of the day, clearly they will need to plan together to divide content and responsibilities.

This may also be a time to start collecting materials. For instance, for Arts Camp: Praise! you will need both paper-towel and wrapping-paper lengths of cardboard tubes, which you will want to begin collecting from the congregation in the spring. Make a list as soon as possible and start asking for these items now so you'll have enough of them.

TWO TO FOUR WEEKS BEFORE CAMP

Final Payments:

Remind parents of the date that final payments for camp are due. It's best to have all payments received at least two to four weeks before Arts Camp begins, as you will need money in your account for food and materials.

You also want to turn in requests for checks for your artists in enough time that you'll be able to pay them at the end of camp.

Order Shirts:

If you are very fortunate, as we are, someone on your artists' team knows a vendor and can take care of this for you. The registration packet for Campers and Counselors asks for shirt sizes, so you should be able to easily compile a list of the shirts you need for all Campers and Counselors, and will only need to ask Instructors and Adult Volunteers.

Pre-Camp Meeting:

About two weeks before Arts Camp begins, meet again with your team. Each member of the team should bring a finalized schedule and a list of specifics as to their plans. These lists should include scriptures, quotes, songs, hymns, projects, games, and anything else each team member plans to use. This will prevent repetition and more importantly allow each of you to build on what the others are doing, making camp flow as naturally as possible. For example, during our Interfaith Camp we learned peace prayers from a variety of spiritual traditions during our Morning Program. Then, during Movement/Drama, we learned a round of chants that incorporated each of these prayers. By the end of the week—and for Arts Camp Sunday—we had a devastatingly beautiful round of peace prayers, led by the Campers, which the entire congregation learned and sang.

Finalize your programming component of camp, and research games that will fit your theme or are known favorites. It's okay for games at the end of the camp day to be more about fun, cooperation, and blowing off steam than to be specifically geared to the theme.

Begin making a shopping list! Wait to buy the lunch food, of course, but starting the list now gives you time to add items as you remember them. There will be food, drinks, and snacks, plus cups and plates and the like. You will also need a list of materials for each day: the storybooks and Bibles you're using and other items. The chapters for each theme provide a list of resources including scripture, books, projects, hymns and songs, and more. It should be the Instructors' responsibility to create the list of materials they need, and everyone should agree on how the purchasing of materials will work. Do the Instructors give you a list, shop, and turn in receipts? Or maybe one day everyone goes material shopping together?

You'll also have a list of items to gather from around the church. I place a large box or crate in my office around this time and start tossing items in it as I think of them.

Organist or Other Accompanist:

You'll want someone who can play piano or guitar, if possible, to accompany the children both for Friday's rehearsal and Sunday's service. Our Associate Rector is an accomplished guitar player, and she has often filled this role for us; our organists are also willing to accompany the children on piano. It's helpful to talk over with whomever will accompany the Campers what the hymns and songs will be, make sure that person has sheet music as needed, and schedule well ahead of time your Friday rehearsal and Sunday warm-up and service.

If you don't have an Accompanist who can join you to run through songs at some point during camp, but will play on Sunday, clear communication between your Camp Director, Music Instructor, and Accompanist becomes all the more critical, and you must make sure everyone is using the same arrangement for every hymn and song.

ONE WEEK BEFORE CAMP

Email Parents and Campers:

Send everyone an email welcoming participants to camp and reminding Campers and parents of dates and start times. You may want to inform parents that Campers should not arrive more than 15 minutes early nor stay more than 15 minutes late every day. Finally, ask that Campers bring a beach towel and a reusable water bottle—both labeled with the Camper's name or initials—on the first day of camp to be left at the church for the week.

You might also encourage parents to dress Campers in clothes—including shoes—that can get painted, marker-ed, dyed, and otherwise messed up!

Meet with Senior Counselors:

Go over the camp schedule and what you'll want them to be doing at different times during the day. Critical times include:

- the first gathering on Monday morning (see the chapter on The Morning Program);
- transitions from one activity/area to another;
- when directions are given for art projects;
- during clean up after art;
- during games.

You also need their help for setup and cleanup every day, so ask them to plan on arriving at 8:40 a.m. and staying until 3:20 p.m..

Sign-In/Sign-Out Sheet:

Create a simple document with a table that includes a row for each Camper's name and 10 columns, two per day (one column per day for parents to initial at dropoff and another column for pickup). Put this on a table wherever Campers will be entering each day, along with blank stickers and a box of thin markers so kids can make a nametag for at least the first two or three days. It's nice to place siblings' names together on the sheet, rather than alphabetizing them, so the adult can find them quickly. We provide a sample Sign-In/Sign-Out Sheet in Appendix 2 (p. 112).

Create Groups:

Unless yours is a very small camp, with fewer than 15 Campers and Counselors combined, you'll want to divide Campers into two groups for the afternoon Music and Movement/Drama time. Each group goes with each Instructor for 45 minutes. Group kids so there is a diversity of ages in each session, and divide Counselors among the groups as well. This is an opportunity to separate siblings as well as pairs who tend to disrupt or ignore the rest when they're together.

For a larger camp with more than 30 participants, you might divide into four groups and adapt the schedule so that two groups are in Art at a time, while the other two cycle through Music and Movement/Drama (you need 1½ hours for Art, while Music and Movement/Drama both work well in a 45-minute session):

	MONDAY	TUESDAY	WEDNESDAY	THURSDAY	FRIDAY
9:45–10:30 Group 1 Group 2 Group 3 Group 4	Art Art Music Movement/Drama	Art Art Music Movement/Drama	Art Art Music Movement/Drama	Art Art Music Movement/Drama	Art Art Music Music
10:30–11:15 Group 1 Group 2 Group 3 Group 4	Art Art Movement/Drama Music	Art Art Music Movement/Drama	Art Art Music Movement/Drama	Art Art Music Movement/Drama	Movement/Drama Movement/Drama Art Art
12:30–1:15 Group 1 Group 2 Group 3 Group 4	Music Movement/Drama Art Art	Music Movement/Drama Art Art	Music Movement/Drama Art Art	Music Movement/Drama Art Art	Prep for Sunday Offering
1:15–2:00 Group 1 Group 2 Group 3 Group 4	Movement/Drama Music Art Art	Movement/Drama Music Art Art	Movement/Drama Music Art Art	Movement/Drama Music Art Art	Prep for Sunday Offering

Lyric Posters:

For every song or hymn you want Campers to learn, make a poster board with the lyrics to that song printed clearly on it. You or an Adult Volunteer[1] will hold these for the kids both at the Friday rehearsal and at the Sunday Offering. This is better than having lyrics in the kids' hands, because it keeps their heads up and visible for parents and parishioners alike. It also helps them stay on track with an adult finger pointing to each line at the right time.

Food Shopping:

Clearly, it's best to do this as close to the day Arts Camp begins as possible. We like to shop on the Friday before camp starts and then deliver everything straight to the church kitchen where we are blessed with a large commercial refrigerator and freezer. If food storage feels impossible, ask parents to pack lunches. Then you can have non-perishable treats or snacks available.

Allergies:

The registration packet asks for this information, so you will be prepared. We keep peanut butter and jelly on a table separate from the rest of the food, and make sure knives that go into the peanut butter do not touch the jelly or anything else. We also provide gluten-free bread and a gluten-free dessert option. For Campers with allergies, we set aside plates marked with their initials and have them make sure they use only those plates all week to avoid unwanted exposure.

Plates and Such:

When we did our "green" themed camp (EcoJustice, Chapter 8), the hypocrisy of using consumable paper products at lunchtime became a glaring problem. That year, we purchased plastic plates that can go in the dishwasher, and began collecting kids' plastic cups from restaurants. Two years ago we received a donation of wonderful sturdy plastic cups from a local realtor who was giving them out at a street fair. We now use those and feel much better about the reduced amount of trash generated by camp lunch.

We put out a dishpan of water with biodegradable soap and some sponges, plus a pan of rinse water, and teach all participants to wash their own plates and cups during the week. We do this outdoors, where the kids like to eat anyway, and volunteers can empty the pans into the garden because of the ecologically safe soap. At the end of camp, the Camp Director or Adult Volunteers take everything home to run through a dishwasher before storing it for the next year.

That's it, you're ready for Arts Camp! Remember above all else to be flexible and keep it fun. Something unexpected will happen every day; a project will go long, a song you thought they'd love will be a bomb, a Counselor will be late, the proverbial creek will rise. You, as the Camp Director, set the tone. If you can laugh off a glitch, take time to solve a problem, and keep it light and compassionate, everyone else will follow your lead.

In the following chapters you will find guidelines for running each portion of the camp day, followed by the resources you need to plan five themed Arts Camps: *Praise!, EcoJustice, Who Is My Neighbor?, Interfaith*, and *Saints and Holy Helpers*. I encourage you to take what's offered and then make it your own.

Happy Camping!

---

[1] The person who is directing the Campers' movements during the Sunday Presentation should be the one doing this, so the children consistently know to look to one adult for direction and guidance.

CHAPTER 3

The Morning Program

	MONDAY	TUESDAY	WEDNESDAY	THURSDAY	FRIDAY
9:00–9:45	Gather and Intros Pray Explore Sing	Gather Pray Review Explore Sing	Gather Pray Review Explore Sing	Gather Pray Review Explore Sing	Gather Pray Review Explore Sing

DURING THIS PART OF THE DAY, YOU INTRODUCE your theme to Campers and use scripture and other sources to explore that theme. This brief morning gathering sets the stage for the day. Having young children sit still too long is always an invitation to misbehavior and inattention, so have them stand to sing and pray. Use introduction games to keep things moving. And don't get bogged down in a discussion that isn't working. Keep a fun song that includes movement up your sleeve for these moments. One of our favorites is "I'm Gonna Sing When the Spirit Says Sing," which you start and then invite kids to offer substitutions for the word *sing,* for example *jump, laugh, shout,* and so forth.

Outside of scripture, a great way to find appropriate quotes and readings is http://www.brainyquote.com. On the site, enter a keyword on your theme in the search bar to find wonderful thoughts on the topic from a variety of thinkers and writers, past and present, religious, sainted, and secular.

Make large readable posters on card stock with your scripture passages and other selections. These will provide some of the focus for your morning explorations. You might hang them all on the wall of your circle space from the beginning of Arts Camp, or you could wait until you've explored them with the Campers and then hang them. Either way is effective. Whenever possible, ask Campers to choose and read both scripture and quotes.

An important part of the morning exploration is your ability to be a storyteller and to generate a discussion with elementary school-aged children. Always try to relate what's been read to the realities of their every-day lives; help them make meaning from scripture that is millennia old. And remember that they are concrete thinkers at this age, and do not dwell comfortably in abstraction or metaphor.

Additionally, you may find some posters already hanging in your classrooms and hallways that expand or complement your theme. Consider borrowing them to hang in your morning space for further focused reflection on the theme.

Monday morning is always a little hectic and confused. As the Camp Director you will need to be at the entrance to greet children and parents, but there are ways to manage everything, especially with good Adult Volunteers and Counselors on hand (prep them ahead of time to help with this):

- If possible, have an Adult Volunteer or Counselor stationed with you at the entrance and another two or three where the children will gather. They can help move Campers to the next space, as well as keep things under control while you're meeting and greeting.

- As you greet—and possibly meet for the first time—parents and caregivers, show them where to sign their Campers in and out every day.
- Have blank nametags and a box of markers available for Campers to make and decorate nametags as they arrive.
- Have a Counselor or Adult Volunteer to show Campers where to place their water bottles (we keep a rolling cart with a five-gallon cooler of ice water on top and space for water bottles on the shelves).
- Have Campers place their folded towels on the floor in a circle: they will use their towel as a place to sit during circle time, and later for meditation and yoga.
- A Counselor or Adult Volunteer who can start a game of I Spy or 20 Questions in the circle while you're delayed with parents is a huge help. Once most Campers have arrived, go to your spot in the circle (near your bookshelf), leaving an Adult Volunteer or Counselor at the sign-up table to greet and guide any late arrivals.

GATHER

If you have a gathering song or hymn that is regularly used in Sunday School, Children's Chapel, or Faith Formation, start singing it. The kids from your parish will join in naturally, and the others will begin to learn it.

We've often used a call and response version of "This Is the Day," by Les Garrett, adapted from Psalm 118:24. This version can be found in the hymnal *Lift Every Voice and Sing II*, #219:

Leader: This is the day
Group: This is the day

Leader: That the Lord has made,
Group: That the Lord has made,

Leader: We will rejoice
Group: We will rejoice

Leader: And be glad in it,
Group: And be glad in it!

All: This is the day that the Lord has made,
We will rejoice and be glad in it!

Leader: This is the day
Group: This is the day

All: That the Lord has made!

Another song appropriate to use every day is "Hallelujah! Praise ye the Lord!" (#179, *Lifesongs*). It functions well as a transition between the Morning Programming and the Art sessions, and can also be used anytime you need Campers to stop what they're doing and attend to you. It is simple enough to be taught quickly; many times we've introduced it to the congregation during the Arts Camp Sunday service. There is a charming video from the early '60s of the Hillcrest Children's Home kids singing this song at: http://www.youtube.com/watch?v=o-86In-qLkYc.

Leader: Hallelu, hallelu, hallelu, hallelujah,
Group: Praise ye the Lord!

Leader: Hallelu, hallelu, hallelu, hallelujah,
Group: Praise ye the Lord!

Leader: Praise ye the Lord!
Group: Hallelujah!

Leader: Praise ye the Lord!
Group: Hallelujah!

Leader: Praise ye the Lord!
Group: Hallelujah!

All: Praise ye the Lord!

Once Campers know this song, break into two groups when you sing it, giving one group the *Leader's* part and the other group the *Group's* part. By Sunday, Campers will be able to invite the congregation to join them, dividing at the center aisle. Campers on the left side lead the left side of the congregation; Campers on the right side lead the right side. (Or divide by men and women, children and adults, and so on.)

You'll have made posters[2] with lyrics for the other songs you plan to use, but your opening song should be one that's simple enough for everyone to learn on the first day. Use this song every day to open camp. You can also use it anytime you want Campers to settle down and refocus.

INTRODUCTIONS

You will likely have a mix of Campers you know well, some you know slightly, and a few you've never met before. To build your unique Arts Camp community, start with the perspective that *everyone* is new. After all, everyone is new to *this* week's experience.

Introductions for children and youth are most comfortable when done in a game. Examples include going around the circle and saying your first name along with your favorite food—or for giggles a food you hate! Another version of this is to say your name and something you like that begins with the same letter (I'm Christina and I like Christmas!). If you have a relaxed group, try standing up and saying your first name and then making a signature move (a fist bump, a clap, a jump, etc.), which everyone then copies while repeating the person's name. Keep it fun and low pressure, and let kids pass if they seem uncomfortable or nervous.

In the following days, skip this step if it isn't necessary, as participants get to know each other.

You can also adapt it as kids become friends:
- Have participants gather together by category. For example: find everyone who is the same age as you; find someone who likes chocolate ice cream; find someone with the same number of siblings as you; etc.
- At some point it may be fun to challenge the kids by asking volunteers to name everyone in the group.

PRAY

Now that you've introduced yourselves, stand in your circle and offer a prayer of Thanksgiving for this week's camp, Campers, Counselors, Instructors, and Adult Volunteers . . . and explorations and adventures. Here is an ancient Buddhist meditation (adapted from singular to plural). It is one that children will take with them after Arts Camp is over, and you can teach them that it is a mantra that can help them calm themselves in a stressful situation.

May we be filled with loving kindness.

May we be well.

May we be peaceful and at ease.

May we be happy.

EXPLORE

Ask the kids what they already know about your theme. Be open to their answers and positive in your response to them. Avoid responses that negate their ideas, no matter how unexpected or random those ideas may seem to you. Instead of "That's not quite what I had in mind," try "I never thought of that before!" "Who can add to that?" is always better than "No. What do you think, Freddy?"

Point to—or pull out if it's not hanging up—the poster with the first scripture passage you've chosen to use (specific recommendations can be found in the chapters for each theme). Ask a volunteer to read it aloud. Try to choose children you know to be proficient and confident readers. Set a rule that if the reader struggles with a word, they may get help from an adult, but other kids will wait patiently and without correcting. If you find you've chosen a struggling reader, simply help that child get to a stopping point and then casually say that it's time to give another child a turn. As the week progresses, there will be time to pull a child aside and practice a short reading

---

[2] Alternately, you can go high tech and use a projector and screen to display lyrics directly from your computer, or low tech and use an overhead projector.

ahead of time, if you have one that clearly wants a turn but needs support.

Once it's been read aloud, check for understanding by asking the kids wondering questions about the reading. Go over any vocabulary they might not know. For example, in Psalm 98, do they know what a *lyre* is and what more common modern instrument might be similar? Then spend time in discussion or even dramatic play to illustrate what the reading means.[3]

Each successive day of Arts Camp, during the Morning Program, you'll ask the Campers what they learned or liked about the day before, then continue your exploration through additional scripture and quotes. Always take time to discuss the readings both for understanding (vocabulary and concepts) and for responses, impressions, and ideas.

End your morning time with a song. There are numerous song suggestions for each of the themed camps in this resource.

Our Instructors come to join us in our circle at this time to begin their session with the Campers. They take charge of moving the Campers to the art space, giving directions, and helping them begin their projects. Use the time while Campers are in these sessions to evaluate the morning session and plan adjustments for the next day, as well as to take pictures of the Campers and their artwork in progress. As the week progresses, more of this time may need to be spent preparing for the Sunday service, but more on that later.

SING

Plan on singing two or three songs during each morning session. Sing to gather and focus the children at the beginning of this time. Sing when you need to change the energy level. Sing to transition from one activity to another.

Song suggestions abound throughout this book, and a comprehensive list of hymnals, songbooks, and websites where you can find music for these songs appears in Appendix 1 (p. 95), with full bibliographic information. In addition, limited bibliographic information is also available in the song list for each themed camp (Chapters 7–11).

---

[3] For each of the themed camps, you will find additional specific information and resources for your Morning Program in their respective chapters.

CHAPTER 4

Art, Music, and Movement/Drama

THIS CHAPTER OUTLINES BEST PRACTICES AND commonalities for these portions of the Arts Camp day. For suggested projects, songs, stories, scripts, and dramatic play specific to each theme, please refer to those chapters. Here are two charts suggesting schedules for Art, Music, and Movement/Drama: one for camps with fewer than 30 combined Campers and Senior Counselors, and another for larger camps.

Schedule for Camps with Less than 30 Campers

	MONDAY	TUESDAY	WEDNESDAY	THURSDAY	FRIDAY
9:45–11:15 All Campers in one group	Art	Art	Art	Art	Art
12:30–2:00 Divide into two groups	Music and Movement/ Drama	Music and Movement/ Drama	Music and Movement/ Drama	Music and Movement/ Drama	Prep for Sunday Offering

Or for a larger (30+) camp:

Schedule for Camps with More Than 30 Campers

	MONDAY	TUESDAY	WEDNESDAY	THURSDAY	FRIDAY
9:45–10:30					
Group 1	Art	Art	Art	Art	Art
Group 2	Art	Art	Art	Art	Art
Group 3	Music	Music	Music	Music	Music
Group 4	Movement/Drama	Movement/Drama	Movement/Drama	Movement/Drama	Music
10:30–11:15					
Group 1	Art	Art	Art	Art	Movement/Drama
Group 2	Art	Art	Art	Art	Movement/Drama
Group 3	Movement/Drama	Music	Music	Music	Art
Group 4	Music	Movement/Drama	Movement/Drama	Movement/Drama	Art
12:30–1:15					
Group 1	Music	Music	Music	Music	Prep for Sunday Offering
Group 2	Movement/Drama	Movement/Drama	Movement/Drama	Movement/Drama	
Group 3	Art	Art	Art	Art	
Group 4	Art	Art	Art	Art	
1:15–2:00					
Group 1	Movement/Drama	Movement/Drama	Movement/Drama	Movement/Drama	Prep for Sunday Offering
Group 2	Music	Music	Music	Music	
Group 3	Art	Art	Art	Art	
Group 4	Art	Art	Art	Art	

We've found that Art easily flows for as many as 24–30 Campers and Counselors combined, while Music and Movement/Drama work best with groups of no more than 15. To do the projects described in this resource, you'll want an hour and a half for Art, while 45 minutes for Movement/Drama and Music are just right. If you use the schedule for large camps, do not introduce a new art project on Friday due to the shortened session. Instead, make this a time for completing projects from the week, looking at finished tie-dye shirts, trading and stringing beads, and doing one last favorite project one more time. Also note that you will combine groups for Movement/Drama and Music, and help your Instructors plan this accordingly. This should be a time for practicing what will happen on Sunday anyway, and bringing the groups together shouldn't be an issue.

Most of the visual art projects are designed to continue over several days, and some can be done more than once (such as beadmaking and God's Eyes). This gives Campers ongoing projects to return to when they've completed something else, allows them to spend more time on favorite activities, and accounts for the varying amounts of time it takes for different children to do the same project. This can be a challenging format for some of us who prefer to start one job and carry it through to completion, but it is most appropriate for encouraging artistic thought and license.

We *strongly* encourage you and your Art Instructors to experiment with each project before you introduce it at camp. This way you'll have an example to share, and you'll have a chance to problem solve before you have a large group of children in front of you!

That said, these are, in most cases, *not* your typical VBS craft projects but rather true artistic process at work. These can be terrifically messy, take more than one session to complete, and do not all come out looking, for the most part, identical. The results will be as unique as your Campers. We encourage you to embrace the mess and imperfection, with the understanding that the richness of your Campers' experience makes it all worthwhile.

In Music, you'll want your Instructor to be prepared with several fun warm-up songs and activities, and to teach the Campers the hymns or songs they'll be presenting on Sunday. Introducing whichever song will be most time consuming on the first day will pay off later in the week. If you have access to instruments—shakers and small drums, rhythm sticks, or even hand bells—and a teacher who can direct kids in their use, they're a great addition to music instruction. For Arts Camp: Who Is My Neighbor?, we used our hand bells and a simple arrangement for "The Servant Song" with a bell choir. For our Saints and Holy Helpers Camp, our Music Instructor David Bell and the Campers together wrote lyrics to the tune of "The Twelve Days of Christmas" and created a new piece called "The Twelve Saints of Arts Camp." The Campers loved adding verses as they learned about Saints all week. For our Interfaith Camp, David brought in his Native American flutes and drums and taught Campers a ceremonial dance. A talented Music Instructor will have the ability and knowledge to make these sessions original and fit them to your parish, but the songs, hymns, and activities we've used are listed in each themed chapter.

For Movement and/or Drama, you'll find a variety of ideas in each chapter. For Praise Camp we used a scripted play, while in the years to follow we've developed more of a collective sermon to share our explorations and discoveries with the parish. To present a scripted Offering, you'll want to begin practicing it during Movement/Drama on Monday and continue every day of camp. For camps that develop a collective sermon type of Offering, we use stories, chants, songs, and games during Movement/Drama and gradually build the Offering the children will bring to Sunday's service. A favorite has been to listen to a story, then use a variety of shawls, scarves, hats, and more from a dress-up box to role-play the story in small groups. Chants and songs can be done in a circle with simple steps and arm motions; kids learn best and are most engaged while moving!

All of your Instructors should be prepared, both physically with materials and supplies and mentally with a strong lesson plan, to take their group(s) and begin instruction and work right away. The Music and Drama Instructors should know a variety of games, warm-ups, and activities to keep positive energy flowing. If you're running a small camp and you wear every hat, take time to plan ahead how you'll transition from one session to the next, and have Adult Volunteers who can have materials set out and ready to go when you and the Campers are ready. If you can, try to move the group among two or more spaces to help with transitions.

SUNDAY'S OFFERING, AS IT RELATES TO DAILY ART, MUSIC, AND MOVEMENT/ DRAMA

Arts Camp Sunday includes an Offering made by the Campers; the Offering is a scripted presentation, often with visuals and/or movement, which campers spend the week preparing to "give" to God and the congregation in the Arts Camp Sunday Worship service. Note that the Offering *is not a performance*. What's the difference? With the Offering (and the entire Arts Camp Sunday service), Campers are there to teach, to share, and to offer what they've explored, created, and discovered with the congregation. We should be cautious, always, about putting children on the altar as performers, which sets them as "other" from the rest of the people in worship. Rather, they have important thoughts and ideas to offer or share, and Arts Camp Sunday is an opportunity for them to do so.

(For more on the appropriateness of emphasizing performance when children lead worship: http://www.buildfaith.org/2012/11/16/the-cuteness-of-children-in-church-not/.)

For this service, we (Campers, Counselors, Instructors, Adult Volunteers, and Camp Director) take over most aspects of the service, including all hymns and readings, the prayers of the people, and the affirmation. Work with your clergy before, during, and after Arts Camp to decide what will work best for your parish.

Whether you use a script or develop one during camp, you'll want a copy for each Camper, with that child's line(s) highlighted for him or her. At St. Barnabas we don't make kids memorize, and they hold their scripts during their offering. We do teach them to hold their script down away from their face, and to try to look up while they read their words. We give them lines they can handle—from their own suggestions—and provide lots of practice throughout the week to help them become comfortable with them.

Scripts or guidelines for the Offering are given for each themed camp. Developing a script or collective sermon from an outline is not as difficult as it may sound, but it does require planning ahead. Have blank paper with you during all of your sessions with the Campers—index cards, a clipboard, a spiral notebook, or whatever works for you. Anytime a child offers a thought or idea on the theme that shows a new understanding, an important discovery, or a sense of connected concepts, stop and write it down along with the child's name. The first few times you do this, you might say something like, "Wait! That was a really important idea you just shared. Let me write it down!" By Thursday, you will hopefully have at least one item from each Camper. If not, just come out and ask the kids for whom you haven't recorded something, "What's something important about our theme that you've discovered at camp this week?" or "What would you like to share about our theme with the people at church on Sunday?" I've had some children choose one of the quotes or Bible passages we read during the Morning Program, which is also fine and easily incorporated into the script by having the child credit the book

and verse, or the thinker, from whom it came. For example, "St. Theresa of Avila was not entirely kidding when she said, 'Lord, deliver me from gloomy saints.'"

As you see, in the end you take all of the ideas the children have given you and add whatever it takes to create a flow. Recruit help for this from your Adult Volunteers and Counselors if needed. You'll need an introduction; an older Camper might be glad to help write and then take responsibility for reading it. You may have favorite scriptures or quotes you want to add; there is almost always at least one Camper who would love to offer more than one item, and we often have several with three or four separate lines in the script. You will also have a young or reserved Camper who feels threatened by the whole idea or simply can't hang onto more than a few words. Once we had a very young six-year-old who offered an enthusiastic, "God is love!" in the middle of the Offering. Obviously, that was perfect!

Complete a final draft before you start the camp day on Friday, with highlighted copies ready for the Campers for the afternoon rehearsal.

Throughout camp, during Morning Program, Music, and Movement/Drama, your team will teach Campers the songs and hymns you've decided to use not only during your Arts Camp Offering, but also throughout the Arts Camp Sunday service. Each camp's specific chapter will clarify and elaborate how this can look and be organized. At St. Barnabas, we have the Campers sing two to four songs and hymns in the body of the Offering, and they offer a hymn or song in place of the Offertory Anthem, as well. For the rest of the service music, while we learn and practice during the week, we invite the congregation to sing with us. This decreases the sense of the Campers as a trained act of performers, and increases the sense that they are a part of our community with a special Offering to share. It also takes a lot of pressure off of Campers and Instructors and engages the congregation!

Again, choose your hymns and songs with your Music Instructor. Make a schedule of which days they'll learn the songs; it makes sense to start on Monday with the ones they'll be singing during their Offering so they will know them well by the end of the week.

You'll note that for camps of any size, the Friday schedule includes time for "Sunday prep." This is the time you'll want your Music and Movement/Drama Instructors, along with your Accompanist, to join you and all the Campers, Counselors, and Adult Volunteers to run through Sunday's service. You may have kids who do not regularly attend church, so briefly outlining everything that will happen from beginning to end is helpful for everyone.

Stop anytime there is a hymn or song, and sing it with your Accompanist. Stop to make adjustments and repairs as necessary, then keep moving. A critical part of this rehearsal time is "blocking." This is deciding where the children will be positioned for different parts on Sunday, and how they move from one space to another. Consider in advance, so you can guide them during rehearsal:

- Are Campers processing at the beginning of the service? If so, where do they enter and where do they go?
- Where will the Campers sit during the service? We use the choir loft, as Arts Camp is always in the summer while the choir is on hiatus. The entire camp, including Counselors and all adults, sits together.
- How will they take their places for the Offering?
- Will they use a microphone? We use a handheld and have found that with preparation it works better than mics on stands. To do this, the children need to be lined up in order of their speaking parts in the Offering. The child doing the introduction is handed the microphone, then each child hands it off to the next one as they go through their presentation. For Campers with more than one line, teach them to move from their first position to the position they need to be in for their next part to be ready for the mic. If they can't do that, then find a way to put all of their lines together in the script. If possible, use blue painter's tape with Campers' names to mark the spot on the floor where they are to stand for the Offering.

For anyone who's ever run a dress rehearsal for a Christmas pageant, this will be familiar, with lots of stops and starts and a certain amount of controlled chaos! But taking this time to work through the challenges and help the Campers prepare will bring great reward on Sunday morning. The more time the adults spend envisioning and problem-solving the logistics beforehand, the better your rehearsal will go. Having an experienced drama teacher and/or actor on your team is immensely helpful with this rehearsal and planning!

Create a printed program for ushers to distribute with the Sunday bulletin. In it, include the names of all Campers, Counselors, Instructors, and Volunteers. Also include a transcript of the Offering, so the congregation can read along in case children mumble or speak too fast. A sample of one of our Arts Camp Sunday programs can be found in Appendix 2 (p. 116).

Send home a note at the end of Friday's camp asking that all Campers and Counselors be at church 30–45 minutes before the service begins on Sunday. You'll use this time to have them put on their camp T-shirts and to practice songs with your Music Instructor and Accompanist. You will always end up with one or two Campers who don't come on Sunday, and they don't always let you know in advance. The registration packet does say that Sunday's service is a part of camp, and that it is hard on the children to be there all week and then miss Sunday, but it still happens. You can prepare the Campers to skip those kids' lines in the script, or get a good reader with confidence to take them over (both Junior and Senior Counselors can be great for this).

Above all, for Friday's rehearsal as well as Sunday's Offering, be calm, flexible, and positive! Mistakes will happen, lines will be botched, a script will be dropped, and more. Smile and remember that the Holy Spirit is present; stay calm and appreciate what the Campers have learned and created in just one week, and they will follow your example of calm positivity.

CHAPTER 5

Story, Grace, Lunch, Playtime, and Meditation/Yoga

	MONDAY	TUESDAY	WEDNESDAY	THURSDAY	FRIDAY
11:15–11:35	Story and Grace	Story and Grace	Story and Grace	Story and Grace	Story and Grace
11:35–12:15	Lunch and Playtime	Lunch and Playtime	Lunch and Playtime	Lunch and Playtime	Lunch and Playtime
12:15–12:30	Meditation/Yoga	Meditation/Yoga	Meditation/Yoga	Meditation/Yoga	Meditation/Yoga

 EVERY DAY THIS TIME WILL LOOK THE SAME. Suggested stories for each day are listed for each themed camp, but you may have a favorite that you'd prefer to use.

Following the morning session of Art or rotations, gather back in your large circle space, with kids sitting on their folded beach towels, making sure they're close enough to see pictures, and introduce and then read your story. Ask children to be thinking about how the story relates to your theme while they listen. Following the Story, you can either have a short wondering time about the story or go straight into Grace and Lunch, depending on time and hunger level.

After the story and any discussion, we stand, hold hands, and say or sing a Grace. One of my favorite sources is *The Barefoot Book of Blessings*. We also like the "Apple Seed Song."

If you don't have a prayer cube, we highly recommend this one: http://www.creatormundi.com/product/the-original-mealtime-prayer-cube/. To use it, pick a child

to roll the prayer cube, then either you or the child reads the prayer aloud.

The following site has an abundance of sung graces, ranging from the funny to the sweet to the deeply spiritual, and all to familiar melodies: http://www.users. ms11.net/~gsong/Graces/firstlines/first.html. (Warning! This site will draw you in for at least a large chunk of time exploring old favorites and new discoveries; it's a great addition to many ministries.)

After they eat, I ask two or three of my Counselors to spread the Campers' beach towels in our large open space; we do this while Campers are finishing Lunch, washing dishes, and playing. We want each child to have a space of his or her own for our meditation and yoga time. We've done this in a circle, but discovered that letting them just spread out works just as well if not better. If you have a large group, having them sit in the lotus position on their towels is fine. If space allows, they can lie down if they desire. Use a singing bowl or chime to call the Campers from lunch to your gathering space. Start meditative yoga or spa music playing before you

 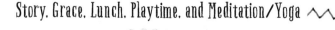

call the Campers, so as they settle they'll begin to hear it. If you know yoga poses, you might want to have children take some of the most calming and opening ones, such as child's pose. Encourage them to breathe slowly and deeply. Centering prayer and Taizé chants can fit well in this time. Or use this brief meditation:

> Close your eyes, and take a slow, deep breath in. Hold that breath . . . and . . . blow it out again. As you breathe in again, feel your body fill with clean, healthful air. Breathe out and feel your feet and legs go completely limp, completely relaxed. Now breathe into your back, fill it with air . . . breathe out and feel your back go totally relaxed. Now breathe into your belly . . . *(and so on until you've calmed the entire body).*

Speak slowly, with a calm and low tone. For wigglers, leave them be unless they are disrupting one another, in which case the best intervention is to quietly go stand very close to them, even place a soft hand on a head or shoulder. Don't make eye contact, but continue what you were doing until the child settles. Stay there if you need to for the rest of the session. Teach Senior Counselors and Adult Volunteers this technique as well in case you have a handful of wiggly Campers.

Give participants time to remain still, with music playing, without anyone's voice. They need this as much as we adults, yet children are rarely encouraged to explore stillness and to look inward.

Bring kids back slowly, inviting them to start by wiggling their fingers and toes, by turning their heads side to side, and by sitting up when they're ready. Give them instructions for the next part of their day while they're still on their towels.

Your Instructors should have joined you by now. Read out the groups (also have the lists hanging up somewhere nearby) and have them join their Instructors.

CHAPTER 6

Ending the Camp Day

	MONDAY	TUESDAY	WEDNESDAY	THURSDAY	FRIDAY
2:00–3:00	Popsicles Games Closing	Popsicles Games Closing	Popsicles Games Closing	Popsicles Games Closing	Popsicles Games Closing

BACK IN THE CIRCLE AREA, OR OUTSIDE IF THAT works, we gather for a snack (usually Popsicles) and a chance to relax. Generally, we spend this time talking about the day and what we learned, or just chatting in small groups. As they finish their snack, they'll be ready to be up and moving again, so timing for starting the Games can be tricky. If you can start giving the directions for a game as the last few kids finish their snack, you'll be ready.

Note that some games need a larger degree of set up. Ask your Counselors or Adult Volunteers to do this while Campers are enjoying their snack. Once the game is underway, Counselors have time for their treat.

A list of games can be found in Appendix 3 (beginning on p. 117).

End the game at about 2:50 and gather everyone in a circle, holding hands (or touching elbows if they prefer). Say a closing prayer, for example:

May the circle be open, but unbroken.

May the love of God be ever in our hearts.

Merry meet and merry part and merry meet again.

We end every day with a song, which we then also use to end the service on Sunday. The one we've loved is "As We Now Go," which is available from the Seasons of the Spirit curriculum:

http://www.seasonsonline.ca/search/results/inventory/Music-Audio/Downloadable-Sheet-Music/As-We-Now-Go. This is an absolutely beautiful ending song and is easy to learn. On Sunday, we sing it once all the way through and then invite the congregation to join in as we all sing it together once more. Please note that for copyright purposes, you should buy as many copies as you need for Instructors and musicians. The children can learn the song without sheet music. Always credit publishers in the service bulletin.

If purchasing "As We Now Go" doesn't work for you, you might use the *Alleluia No. 1* (#178, *The Hymnal 1982*) instead, teaching a new verse each day and singing the entire hymn on Friday. Or perhaps your parish or your children's ministry already has a favorite closing song that will work and that the congregation might like to learn on Arts Camp Sunday.

Note: The song "As We Now Go" is actually titled "As We Go Now," but appears on the *Seasons* website as "As we Now Go." Keep this in mind if *Seasons* corrects this error; the link may change.

CHAPTER 7

Arts Camp: Praise!

What is praise?
When do we praise?
How do we praise?
Why do we praise?

THESE QUESTIONS GUIDE THIS VERSION OF ARTS Camp, and the praise theme allows for lots of music, joy, and laughter. By the end of the week, we remember that praise is something we all do in our own way, something we do together at worship, and often something we do when we don't even realize we're doing it!

MORNING PROGRAM

Open camp each day with a simple song. Call and response songs work best because they draw the group in; we recommend "This Is the Day" or "Hallelujah! Praise ye the Lord!" (See Appendix 1, p. 95, for more on music and where to find the songs recommended throughout this chapter.) Since these songs will be part of Arts Camp Sunday Worship, you want Campers to know these songs inside and out by the end of the week. You will also be *closing* the Morning Program with a song, so you can use both of the above options every morning.

Mentions of praise in scripture are, of course, numerous. Suggested verses include but are not limited to:

- Psalm 98:4–6
- Psalm 100
- Psalm 148
- Psalm 150
- Isaiah 42:10–12
- 1 Chronicles 16:31–33
- Matthew 22:37–39
- 1 Corinthians 12:4–11
- Philippians 4:4–8
- Judges 5:6, 11 (These verses are lifted completely out of context. If that's uncomfortable for you, feel free to omit them!)

Once a Camper has read the day's scripture, ask wondering questions about what they heard. Check for understanding of the main idea, as well as for vocabulary that might need explaining. Continue the conversation by asking:

- How can we praise?
- When do we praise?
- Whom do we praise?

As the week progresses, dive into the variety of ways we praise God as well as the not-so-obvious ways we praise God, for instance, sharing a treat with another child might be a form of praise, as might running in circles and giggling just because it feels good. God gave us these amazing bodies, and when we use them with a feeling of freedom, joy, and abandon, we praise their Creator.

Spend time talking about the ways in which your parish and your faith tradition praise God. Invite children who may have joined you from other parishes or from families without a parish home to share what they know of praise.

Once you've read and discussed the scripture passage(s) for the day, close your session with a song before transitioning to Art (or Art, Music, and Movement/Drama if you have a large camp).

At any point during the morning's explorations, you can use songs to change the energy or to fill time. Songs like "This Little Light of Mine" and "Arky Arky" are perfect for these moments (although, if you sing all the verses to "Arky Arky," plan on about 10 solid minutes!).

Hymns and Songs

- "All Things Bright and Beautiful" (#405, *The Hymnal 1982*)
- "Joyful, Joyful, We Adore Thee" (#376, *The Hymnal 1982*)
- "Alleluia No. 1" (#178, *The Hymnal 1982*)
- "This Is the Day" (#219, *Lift Every Voice and Sing*)
- "Hallelujah! Praise ye the Lord!" (#179, *Lifesongs*)
- "This Little Light of Mine" (#32, 33, *Lifesongs*)
- "Give Me Oil in My Lamp" (#158, *Lifesongs*)
- "Arky Arky" (http://www.hymnary.org/hymn/SWM/66
- "Halle, Halle, Hallelujah!" (#177, *Lifesongs*)
- "Amen, Siakudumisa" (http://www.choristersguild.org)
- "As We Now Go" (http://www.seasonsonline.ca/search/results/inventory/Music-Audio/Downloadable-Sheet-Music/As-We-Now-Go) *or* "Alleluia #1" (#178, *The Hymnal 1982*)
- "Mr. Sun" (See our original lyrics in the Praise! script. You can learn the melody here: http://www.songsforteaching.com/folk/ohmrsun.php)

Please note that "Hallelujah! Praise ye the Lord!" and "Halle, Halle, Hallelujah" are two different songs, both very appropriate to the theme of praise and both a lot of fun to learn and sing. They can both be found in the songbook *Lifesongs* from Augsburg Fortress.

ARTS CAMP SUNDAY

Planning

Plan your Arts Camp Sunday Worship service with clergy and other parish staff. We recommend that Leaders and Campers present the following portions of the service, which includes incorporating the prepared Offering. Our rector gives us the sermon time for the Arts Camp offering every year; work with your clergy to decide what is best for your parish.

Here are our recommendations for the service:

Entrance Hymns (Campers only):
- "Halle, Halle, Hallelujah!"
- "Give Me Oil in My Lamp"

Note: Campers sing "Halle, Halle, Hallelujah!" once through, then segue immediately into "Give Me Oil in My Lamp" while processing in just as the choir normally would.

Hymn of Praise (Campers and Congregation):
- "This Is the Day" (In place of the "Gloria")

Sequence Hymn (Campers and Congregation):
- "All Things Bright and Beautiful"

Offertory Anthem (Campers and Congregation):
- "Joyful, Joyful, We Adore Thee"

Communion Hymn (Campers only):
- "Amen, Siakudumisa"

Closing Hymn:
- "As We Now Go"
- "Alleluia No. 1"

Note: Choose either of these for the final hymn. If you use "As We Now Go," have Campers sing both verses to the congregation, then invite the congregation to sing both verses with you to conclude the service. Remember to close camp each day with whichever song you choose for the end of Sunday's service.

Music during the Arts Camp Offering:
- "Mr. Sun"
- "Hallelujah! Praise ye the Lord!"

Readings

With clergy approval, we recommend the following readings for the Liturgy of the Word during Arts Camp Sunday Worship:

- Old Testament: Isaiah 42:10–12
- Psalm: Psalm 148
- New Testament: Philippians 4:4–8
- Gospel: Matthew 22:37–39

Invite Campers who are confident readers and speakers to volunteer to read at the service, and have the readings ready for them to take home to practice. On Friday, while rehearsing, show these readers how to approach the altar, where to stand while reading, how to adjust a microphone if that's needed, and how to leave the lectern after they've read. Do have them practice the actual reading as well, and stop to coach for any pronunciation or vocabulary difficulties. Write phonetic pronunciations or reminders on their copies to help them.

Make sure clergy and the parish administrator know that Campers will do the readings on Arts Camp Sunday, so other parish volunteers aren't asked to do so. Also, music and lyrics for songs the congregation is invited to sing together with the Campers should be listed or printed in the service bulletin.

Eucharistic Prayer 6, from the Welsh Book of Common Prayer (http://crucix.com/welsh/communion/cinw-hc-english.pdf, beginning on page 67), is fitting on Arts Camp Sunday.

PRE-LUNCHTIME STORIES

- Monday: *Let the Whole Earth Sing Praise* by Tomie dePaola
- Tuesday: *Because Nothing Looks Like God* by Lawrence and Karen Kushner and Dawn W. Majewski
- Wednesday: *God in Between* by Sandy Eisenberg Sasso and Sally Sweetland
- Thursday: *All the World* by Liz Garton Scanlon and Marla Frazee
- Friday: *Light the Candle! Bang the Drum!* by Ann Morris and Peter Linenthal

GRACE

See Chapter 5, page 33 for a variety of resources.

ART

Sun Sculptures

Concept:

God created the light and the dark, and it was good! God is light! The light of Christ shines on all of us! And what better symbol of light than the sun? The light of the sun makes flowers and all things grow.

Materials:

- Crayola Model Magic®
- chopsticks
- yarn
- paint: gold or yellow, plus black, blue, red, green for faces
- paintbrushes: various small sizes
- newspaper or butcher paper to cover work spaces

Directions:

1. At least 24–36 hours prior to the start of Praise Camp, use the following instructions to create a sample Sun Sculpture, including allowing it to dry and painting it. Bring this sample to the activity, and show it to participants so they can see how their sculptures will harden.

2. As you begin the activity, demonstrate how to make one sun sculpture while the kids watch. Model Magic® is fun and easy to use, and kids can shape and reshape their suns until they're happy with them. The most important part of your demonstration is to show them how thick to make the suns: about ½ to 1 inch. Thicker and they will become heavy and more likely to fall off the stick and break. Thinner and they will break around the stick when they dry or as the kids hold them. On Monday participants form their Sun Sculptures and push a chopstick into the bottom for a handle.

3. Provide a large board or cookie trays set aside for participants to lay finished suns down to dry; you won't want to do anything with them until Wednesday, when kids can paint one side.

4. On Thursday participants will be able to finish their Sun Sculptures by painting the backside.

5. On Friday they will be able to rehearse with their Sun Sculptures (see the section on Movement/Drama, p. 44).

Personal Flags or Banners

Concept:

It's a good idea to have several samples or pictures of banners to show the kids.

People all over the world, over the centuries, have created banners and flags to show what's important to them. Churches love banners (show the children the ones in your building, if possible). Kingdoms and nations have their own special flags; families had shields with symbols and pictures that show their strengths and values; colleges and universities have triangular pennants with their name or initials to wave at football games. Each of the Apostles has his own shield, and so does The Episcopal Church.

This week you will get to make your own banner or flag. Use it to show something special about who you are and what's important to you. Create it to show praise for your life, your family, yourself, and your relationship with God. Today we will plan these on paper so you can make changes and adjustments, then tomorrow you can start creating your banner on a piece of cloth.

Materials:

- paper that approximately matches the size of cloth you've chosen
- pencils and erasers
- cloth pieces: old sample books, felt, or just squares of muslin work well
- felt or foam for cutouts: widely available at craft stores
- markers: a variety of thin and wide tip
- yarn in a variety of colors and sizes
- scissors that will cut cloth as well as yarn
- dowels
- glue: washable school glue to secure cloth and yarn to their flags, plus a hot glue gun operated by an adult to affix the dowel to the finished product

Directions:

1. Fold one side of your paper about 1" from the edge, and then turn it over, keeping the fold. The folded part will be where your banner wraps around a pole, so you don't want to put pictures and words on this part.

2. Think about symbols, shapes, and pictures that say something important about you, your family, your relationship with God, and how you praise God. You can choose to divide your paper into different sections as on a medieval shield, or mix all your ideas together like on a flag.

3. Draw the pictures and shapes you want on your banner or flag. You can add words, too, if you like. Once you have a design you like, make sure your name is on the paper and turn it in. We'll give it back to you tomorrow with the cloth and other materials to start your flag.

4. On Tuesday and over the remaining days, you will provide Campers with the felt and foam, yarn, and markers to complete their banners. In addition to drawing with markers, they can make shapes and more using foam, felt, and yarn, and glue them onto

the cloth. Make sure they remember to keep about an inch clear for the flagpole you'll be adding at the end.

5. Once banners are finished, have an Adult or Senior Counselor spread a curvy line of hot glue into the undecorated side of the flag, then roll a dowel into the cloth until the dowel is completely covered. Add a line of hot glue to secure the cloth to itself, if necessary.

Banner for Sunday Offering

Concept:

This will be a larger, camp-wide version of the personal banners they're making. This banner will also be the backdrop and a prop for the Arts Camp Sunday Offering.

Materials:

- markers
- a large piece of cloth, approximately 6' x 2'–3'
- cord or strong string
- a hot glue gun or sewing materials (you will do this before camp begins)

Directions:

1. Before camp begins, write the word *PRAISE* across the center of your banner in large, easily readable, block letters. You might add an exclamation point for emphasis. You want the insides of the letters to be empty so Campers can color them.

2. Sew or hot glue a cord, string, or long dowel into the top edge of the banner so you'll be able to hang it in the sanctuary. We hung ours from the front of the altar. You'll want it to be highly visible for Sunday, as it is a part of the Campers' Offering.

3. As you're giving instructions on Monday, show Campers where they can find this banner and the markers to use on it. Tell them that anytime they have finished another project, or are waiting for an Adult Volunteer or Counselor's help, they can come over and add praise-related words or pictures to the banner or help to color in the letters. Make sure it's understood that everything that goes on the banner should be centered on praise and thankfulness (this isn't the place for that awesome alien-eats-family picture they've been perfecting!).

4. Leave this banner out until Friday, when it should be hung in the sanctuary before rehearsal time.

Rain Sticks

Concept:

We praise God for the rain that helps things live and grow! People in Central America use rain sticks to make a joyful noise.

Materials:

- paper-towel tubes: ask parishioners to bring these in a few weeks in advance
- construction paper in a variety of colors
- strips of colored paper, 1"–2" thick
- markers and crayons
- masking tape
- white glue or glue sticks
- dried lentils/peas/beans/rice
- funnels or paper shaped as a funnel

Directions:

Note: Demonstrate this project to Campers before sending them to make theirs.

1. Cut two circles larger than the end hole of the tube out of construction paper. You can do this by simply standing the tube on the paper and tracing a large circle.

2. Place one circle over one end, and gently squeeze it so the overlapping area folds down over the tube. It will wrinkle; smooth it as much as you can but don't worry too much about some wrinkles. Use the masking tape to secure the paper firmly to the cardboard of the tube, and to create a smooth surface where the paper meets the tube.

3. Decorate a piece of 9" x 12" construction paper with markers and crayons. Make it festive and colorful! Lay the paper facedown on the table and spread white glue on 3 of the 4 edges and in the middle. Stop gluing about 1" from the 4th edge.

4. Use a funnel (or shape a piece of paper into a funnel) to pour a few handfuls of dried lentils, peas, beans, and/or rice into the tube. Use another paper circle to cover the remaining end, and secure it tightly with

masking tape. Kids can either color the masking tape or use a strip of colored paper to cover it.

5. Place the second circle over the open end of the tube and fold the overlap to cover the end. Again, smooth wrinkles as best as you can and then use masking tape to secure the paper.

6. Decorate the masking tape with permanent markers, or glue a colorful strip of paper over it to hide it. (Campers can use the strips to make stripes on their rain stick as well, of course.)

7. Tip the rain stick slowly to make a gentle rain sound; shake it or tip it faster to make a stronger sound!

Didgeridoos or Balloon Flutes

Concept:
The indigenous people of Australia have used didgeridoos to make a joyful noise during important ceremonies and celebrations. These balloon versions are super fun, once kids have mastered playing them.

Materials:
* wrapping-paper tubes (*Start collecting these from the parish starting at Christmastime!*)
* balloons (*Because they can tear, have lots of extras!*)
* butcher paper in a few colors
* markers and crayons
* masking or duct tape
* glue or glue sticks

Directions:
Note: Make sure you make a sample of this project in advance, and practice until you have the feel for how to play it!

1. Have kids decorate their tubes first, either by coloring the tubes themselves or coloring and then cutting and gluing a piece of butcher paper onto it.

2. Campers then come to an Adult Volunteer or Counselor for the balloon: cut the open end of the balloon off, leaving enough balloon to fit over the tube opening with plenty of extra to pull down around the end.

3. Pull the edges down at least an inch or two, so the balloon fits tightly over the opening, and secure all the way around it with tape.

4. Put your mouth in the other opening, with your lips pressed together, and blow hard to make a joyful noise! This takes a few tries for some kids while others get it right away. Have them help each other!

God's Eyes

Concept:
Do you remember twining yarn around a stick cross to make these when you were a kid? We did, and it was a joy to see our Campers enjoying the results as much as we used to. We couldn't get some of them to stop, and had them weaving during storytime and even lunchtime! One of our most wiggly and active boys made over a dozen beautiful God's eyes in different colors and sizes.

Materials:
* yarn in lots of different colors
* chop sticks (*We've found restaurant supply stores that sell these in bulk, and we stock up every year.*)
* craft sticks

Directions:
Note: You might show Adult Volunteers and Counselors ahead of time how to start the God's eye by forming a cross, then they'll be ready to help, and all of the Campers will be able to begin more quickly.

1. Wrap yarn once or twice around the middle of one stick, securing the loose end under the wrap.

2. Hold the sticks perpendicularly against each other: like a cross but crossing at the midpoint of each stick.

3. Wrap the yarn in a criss-cross pattern around the two sticks until they are securely held together in shape; about 8–12 times.

4. Begin to wrap in a pattern, going around the back of one stick and the front of the next . . . back, front, back, front.

5. Continue, moving the yarn out gradually so that each strand sits next to the one before it, until the desired size is reached. Some of our kids liked the look of

having an inch or so of chopstick bare, while others wanted to wrap the yarn all the way to the ends.

6. Keep going to the end, secure the yarn by tying a knot, and cut it with a few inches left to tie a loop to hang the God's eye.

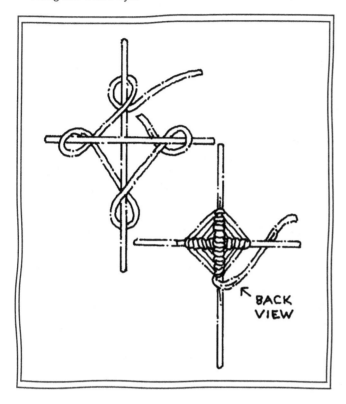

BACK VIEW

Tie-Dye

Note: We do this for every Arts Camp!

Concept:

Our shirts bring us together as a community. Each starts the same, then proclaims how each of us is our own special and unique child of God. No two will ever look alike once they've been dyed! We thank God for camp, for color, for the magic that happens when we combine colors and when we appear to make a mess. We present these shirts to each other, to the congregation, and to God on Sunday when we make our Offering at worship. And we keep the shirts, some of us year after year, to remember the joy, faith, fun, and fellowship of each year's camp.

Materials:

- T-shirts; preordered from a printer (see Chapter 2: *2–4 Weeks before Camp,* p. 18)
- rubber bands for tying shirts
- dye kit including squirt bottles *(These are neater and safer than vat dyeing!)*
- gallon plastic zipper bags
- paint shirts or trash bag ponchos to cover kids *(optional)*
- non-latex gloves
- tarps
- crates: With 24–28 enrollment, we use two crates.
- large tubs, big enough to hold 2 overturned crates with a bit of room between

Notes:

- We use and highly recommend dyes, fixers, and instructions from Grateful Dyes Inc. They have everything you need plus great instructions, and they ship worldwide. Here is their website: http://www. grateful-dyes.com.
- You can also find tie-dye kits at most hobby stores. Make sure you buy a kit that comes with specific instructions and includes the fixers you need to mix the dyes. You'll want to have everything ready to go when the kids dye their shirts, including three squirt bottles per station with red, yellow, and blue dye. Some kits have you soak shirts in a solution prior to dying; you'll want your Art Instructors and Counselors to make sure this is done ahead of time.
- Instructions and diagrams for dyeing shirts in specific patterns are available from Grateful Dyes as well as all over the Internet!

Directions:

Note: We do this outside on the lawn and still spread tarps . . . this is a messy activity! Putting the tied shirts on an overturned milk crate that in turn is standing in a large metal tray or plastic tub helps catch excess dye. Before you begin, have Counselors mark each shirt with the Campers' initials; you should have compiled a list when you ordered, using the Campers' registration packets to determine each child's size.

1. On Monday, once other Art projects are well under way, take small groups and hand out their shirts. Show kids how to twist their shirts and then secure them with rubber bands, helping them as needed.

2. Store the tied shirts in a large tub.

3. On Tuesday and/or Wednesday, have a tie-dye station set up outdoors, close to a door that leads to the art space, if possible. You want at least 1 Adult Volunteer and a Counselor for every 4 Campers that are tie-dying.

4. Have Campers put on gloves, and paint shirts or ponchos if desired.

5. Give Campers their tied shirts and have them place them on one of the overturned milk crates in the tub.

6. Using 1 color at a time, use the squirt bottles to saturate the part of the shirt where you want that color. If you want a very colorful shirt, you need to really soak the area.

7. Repeat step 6 using different colors on the rest of the shirt.

8. Turn the shirt over and repeat steps 6 & 7 on this side (if children want their shirts to be similar on both sides have them turn them over as they do each color and section).

9. Place the finished shirt in a gallon zipper bag and seal it.

10. The Art Instructors will need to rinse the shirts and then run them through a washing machine before they're finished. For a large camp we suggest that the adults all take a batch of shirts home and help out!

11. *Hold on to the shirts until Sunday!* We always show the kids their finished shirts on Friday, but then collect them again to hand out on Sunday morning.

MUSIC

Monday through Thursday, your Music Instructor will be teaching Campers the songs for Sunday. They'll learn "This Is the Day" and "As We Now Go" (or the "Alleluia No. 1") during morning programming and the daily closing, and they'll learn "Mr. Sun" during drama, so the songs they should learn during music are:

- "Halle, Halle, Hallelujah"
- "Give Me Oil in My Lamp"
- "Amen, Siakudumisa"
- "Joyful, Joyful, We Adore Thee"

It works well to start on Monday with the trickiest piece, which your Music Instructor should decide. Then on Tuesday review that song and introduce another. On Wednesday review both songs and begin another. Thursday, introduce the last song, which should be the one deemed easiest to learn, and then practice all of them. On Friday you'll run through every song during the Sunday prep or rehearsal time. Have posters with clearly written lyrics for each song, which decreases paper use (and potential loss and destruction!), and keeps children's heads up while they're singing, rather than having them buried in a songbook. A Counselor can manage and hold the posters during Music.

Again, the music session should also include some songs that are just for fun and some song-related games. Campers will quickly tire of learning song after song.

For resources, check http://www.ultimatecampresource.com. One of our favorites is the "Button Factory Song." They also have songs in rounds, grace songs, and more songs with movements.

MOVEMENT/DRAMA

Movement/Drama will focus on the scripted Offering all week. Don't hand out scripts on the first day. Instead, after a warm-up exercise or game, take the Campers into the sanctuary and introduce the story line to them as a brief run-through. Include both songs from the script, including any movements they will do. They won't have their completed suns, rain sticks, or didgeridoos yet, but it's a good idea to have them pretend to use them. On Tuesday, following a warm-up, ask for volunteers who want particular parts:

- *Camper 1* is a large role with many lines, so recruit an older child who is a good reader and confident speaking in front of people.
- The *Narrator, Leper 1,* and *Jesus* should likewise be confident readers and speakers.
- The role of the other *Lepers* appeals to many kids because of the yuck factor.
- Everyone else fills in as the *Campers.*

Note that there are lines enough here for a very large camp, but smaller camps can give Campers more than one line. Before giving highlighted scripts to Campers, decide on roles and replace the word *Camper* with the name of the child reading the line.

Also note, there is space to individualize the script; feel free to replace lines with ideas from your Campers, and/or to add their original lines.

When we made this Offering, we had 4 microphones on stands spread across the front of the altar. On Friday during our rehearsal time, kids learned which microphone they needed to go to when it was time for their spoken parts. They also learned to step back and make space for other Campers to do their lines. Before Friday's rehearsal, the Drama Instructor and Camp Director should work together to plan which microphone each camper will use (we mark them "Mic 1," "Mic 2," etc.), with thought to how the Offering will best flow. You will need to work with your parish's sound team to set up and run the microphones for Friday's rehearsal as well as Sunday's Offering.

The script for the Offering can be found at the end of this chapter.

POPSICLES/SNACK, GAMES, AND CLOSING THE CAMP DAY

See Chapter 6 (p. 35) for how to end the day and Appendix 3 (p. 117) for a list of tried-and-true camp games.

FRIDAY AFTERNOON

Before you pray and sing, which should be the last act of the last day of Arts Camp, you may want to leave time for an evaluation. A simple evaluation form can be found in Appendix 2 (p. 114).

You'll also want to make sure Campers take home the things they brought with them at the beginning of the week and that have accumulated throughout camp: water bottles, beach towels, sweaters and sweatshirts, hats and sunglasses. Also send home any art projects that you do *not* want to use or display on Sunday. Keep tie-dye shirts and everything else they will wear or display Sunday.

You'll want your Art Instructor(s) and Counselors to spend time following the last Art session on Friday setting up a display of the Campers' creations so that is in place for Sunday.

Finally, send a note home with each family on Friday afternoon thanking them for bringing their children to camp and giving them details on the Sunday service, including what time Campers should arrive. You want time for Campers to put on their tie-dye shirts and to come to the choir loft to practice before the service begins. A sample of this note home can be found with the forms in Appendix 2 (p. 113). We copy this note on brightly colored paper and place it next to the sign-out sheet for parents to see and take when they come to pick up their Campers.

As with every day of Arts Camp, but especially on Friday, you'll want your Counselors to stay later so they can help you put camp away!

Throughout the week, we have parents who tend to arrive to pick up their children a little early, so they've seen and heard our closing prayer and song. On Friday, once we've given instructions for taking things home and final cleanup, invite parents and caregivers to join the circle at this time. Then try not to get emotional as you sing your goodbye blessing and realize that Arts Camp is over for the year.

ARTS CAMP SUNDAY OFFERING SCRIPT

by Rachel Turner

Used with permission.

Note: In the script below, "Any Camper" means that these lines can be assigned to different participants; spread them around! "Camper 1," on the other hand, is the same participant throughout the script.

Camper 1: *(enters church and walks up to Praise banner, then reads aloud)* Praise. Hmmm . . . what is Praise?

(More Campers appear.)

Any Camper: I'm glad you asked! Praise means many different things.

Camper 1: *(surprised by others)* Whoa! Where did all of you come from? What is this place?

Any Camper: This is a church. This is a place where people gather together to worship and praise God.

Camper 1: Oh, okay. But what do you mean by "praise"?

Any Camper: It means to tell about God, and how wonderful and awesome and great God is!

Camper 1: Uh, okay, but . . . doesn't God already know that? I mean, God is . . . God.

Any Camper: Yes, but when we praise God, it brings us closer to him.

Any Camper: Like when we sing "Glory to God in the highest," we understand more and more about God's power and love, and we feel closer to God.

Camper 1: Okay, I think I understand. So, what else can we do to praise God?

(More Campers enter.)

Any Camper: We can praise God by giving thanks.

Camper 1: *(suspiciously)* Wait a second, it's not November and I don't see any turkey.

Any Camper: *(laughing)* It doesn't have to be Thanksgiving for us to give thanks! God wants us to do that all year long.

Any Camper: Thank you, God, for books and food!

Any Camper: Thank you, God, for friends and family!

Any Camper: Thank you, God, for music!

Any Camper: Thank you, God, for making me!

Any Camper: Thank you, Lord, for the rain!

(Campers hold up their rain sticks and make a "rain storm.")

Any Camper: Thank you, Lord, for the sun!

(Campers put down rain sticks, hold up their suns. Accompanist plays brief intro to "Mr. Sun" while all Campers sing.)

> Creator God made everything around;
> The sun, the stars, and me. (repeat)
>
> We thank you, Lord, for giving us,
> the big bright golden sun.
>
> We give you praise, praise; praise to our Lord,
> God shines right through me. (repeat)
>
> We thank you, Lord, for loving us,
> We have all we need!
>
> We give you praise, praise; praise to our Lord,
> God shines right through . . .
> God shines right through . . .
> God shines right through me.
>
> Ba doo ba doo, yeah!

Camper 1: *(still singing quietly)* Ba doo, ba doo, yeah! Wow! That was great! I didn't know praising God could be fun!

Any Camper: Of course! Psalm 100 says, "Make a joyful noise to the Lord all the earth."

Any Camper: "Worship the Lord with gladness!"

Any Camper: "Come into God's presence with singing!"

Camper 1: Awesome!

Any three Campers together: Exactly!

Camper 1: Okay, so I think I understand what praise is, but when do you do it? When you're here, in church?

Any Camper: Yes, coming to church is a way to make time to praise God.

Any Camper: But that's not the only time.

Any Camper: God wants us to praise Him all the time . . .

Any Camper: When we eat a meal,

Any Camper: When the sun is shining and the world looks happy,

Any Camper: But also when you're feeling sad.

Any Camper: We can, and should, praise anytime, anywhere, and any place!

Any Camper: We can read in the Bible about people who gave praise; and some people who forgot!

Narrator: *(This child's copy of the script has a fake cover that says "Children's Bible" in large letters.)* One day when Jesus (enter Jesus) was traveling to Jerusalem, he met 10 men who all had leprosy. (Enter 10 lepers, looking ill and bedraggled.) They stood at a distance and called out in a loud voice.

Lepers: *(all together)* Jesus, Master, have pity on us!

Camper 1: Whoa, whoa, wait a sec . . . what is lepruh . . . lepruh . . .

One leper steps forward and says, in a scientific voice . . .

Leper 1: Leprosy is a chronic infectious disease caused by mycobacterium affecting the skin and nerves with the formation of nodules that enlarge, spread, and cause loss of sensation, wasting of muscle, and production of deformities.

All: *(including other lepers)* Ewwwwwww!

Leper 1: What? That's what it is.

Leper 2: You can see why we want to be healed.

Camper 1: Yeah, I'm getting that!

Narrator: *(impatient, trying to get everyone back to the story)* They stood at a distance and called out in a loud voice,

Lepers: *(all together)* Jesus, Master, have pity on us!

Narrator: When Jesus saw them he said,

Jesus: Go, show yourselves to the priests. *(Enter two priests on either side. Lepers split into two groups and go to priests. Priests make the sign of the cross over each leper.)*

Narrator: And as they went they were cleansed. *(Lepers look at hands and arms and are amazed and happy. Nine exit without a glance back at Jesus. One remains.)*

Grateful Leper: Hallelujah! Praise be to God!

Narrator: He threw himself at Jesus' feet and thanked him.

Grateful Leper: Thank you, Jesus!

Any Camper: And he was a Samaritan.

Camper 1: *(raising his/her hand)* Um . . . Samaritan?

Any Camper: A Samaritan was a foreigner who was also an outcast in this area.

Any Camper: Jesus asked,

Jesus: Were not all 10 cleansed? Where are the other nine? Did no one return and give praise to God except this foreigner? Rise and go; your faith has made you well.

(Jesus and Leper hug and both exit.)

Camper 1: Wow . . . so only one person out of the 10 that Jesus healed came back to say thank you, to give praise?

Any Camper: Yes it's true. Sometimes it is hard to remember to praise God.

Any Camper: But God loves when we praise Him all the time.

Any Camper: When we praise God, we can feel close to our Creator and remind ourselves how great and wonderful God is!

Any Camper: We praise God, because God is always worthy of praise.

All: Alleluia!

Camper 1: So now I know what praise means, and I know that we can praise God all the time, but how do we do it?

Any Camper: There are so many ways to praise God, we can't even count them! We read in First Corinthians:

Any Camper: "There are different ways to serve the same Lord, and we can each do different things. Yet the same God works in all of us and helps us in everything we do."

(Here you can insert Campers' ideas of how we praise.)

Any Camper: We can praise God by loving our neighbor.

Any Camper: Jesus said, "You shall love the Lord your God with all your heart, and with all your soul, and with all your mind. This is the greatest and first commandment."

Any Camper: "And the second is like it: You shall love your neighbor as yourself."

(Possibly insert more Camper ideas here.)

Any Camper: Praise God with trumpet sound!

(All take out and blow balloon trumpets.)

Any Camper: Make a joyful noise to the Lord, all the earth.

(All sound balloon trumpets.)

Any Camper: Let everything that has breath praise the Lord!

(All sound trumpets for one last, long, loud blast!)

(Break into song for the finale: "Hallelujah! Praise ye the Lord!")

CHAPTER 8

Arts Camp: EcoJustice

What does God desire of us when it comes to our care of creation?

Why is stewardship of the earth a faith-based issue?

What can we do to live in harmony with and help protect all of God's creation?

HESE QUESTIONS FOCUS OUR WEEKLONG EcoJustice Camp. We also explore the components of creation itself, using the book of Genesis as our starting point. The *Abundant Life Garden Project,* written by Cynthia Coe and available from Episcopal Relief and Development, delves into five components of creation: *water, seeds, soil, animals,* and *harvest.* Download the lessons for each of these components here:

http://www.episcopalrelief.org/ church-in-action/christian-formation/ christian-formation-for-children#Abundant.

We used the lessons and activities from the *Abundant Life Garden Project* for our Morning Program and Games, then filled in with our own Art, Music, and Movement/Drama.

MORNING PROGRAM

Remember to have the sign-in/sign-out sheet ready for parents and caregivers, and nametags and markers for all Campers for the morning check-in time.

Gather and begin with a song. "This is the Day" fits the theme and will be used in Arts Camp Sunday Worship. Additionally, here are other fun choices, with the first two also being recommended for the Sunday service:

- "The Garden Song" (http://www.irish-folk-songs. com/the-garden-song-lyrics-chords-and-sheet-music.html)
- "I'm Gonna Sing" (*Lift Every Voice and Sing II,* #117)
- "Arky Arky" (http://www.hymnary.org/hymn/ SWM/66)

The *Abundant Life Garden Project* lessons have everything you need for your Morning Program, including prayers, group activities, and guiding questions. In fact, they have enough for twice the time scheduled, so choose which pieces best fit your parish, your teaching style, and your camp. You might save the stories from these lessons for your pre-lunch story time, although we've also offered other great books to read.

You'll also need a copy of a charming book called *Whole World,* by Christopher Corr and Fred Penner, available from Barefoot Books, which contains updated lyrics to Margaret Bond's classic song, "He's Got the Whole World in His Hands," shifting the responsibility for stewardship firmly onto all of us. The book is filled with wonderful illustrations, a "Did you know" section in the back, and a simple version of sheet music and lyrics for the song. Barefoot Books also has a video cartoon of the song (uploaded to YouTube here: http://www.youtube.com/ watch?v=ODftYTD3Rbs), which you can show to introduce the book for both Art and Drama.

For our EcoJustice camp, we did adjust the order of the *Abundant Life Garden Project* lessons, and added the *Whole World* book:

- *Monday: Animals*

On Monday morning show the video of *Whole World* (again, found at http://www.youtube.com/watch?v=ODftYTD3Rbs). You could do this at the end of the Morning Program or at the beginning of Art, but Campers will need to see it before they begin painting their African drums. If not viewing the video, simply read the book and look together at the illustrations.

Also on Monday, a parishioner who is a master gardener came in with a worm box and taught about composting. We then used the worm box for our lunch leftovers, according to her instructions, for the rest of the week. Reminder: always be on the lookout for parishioners with expertise and invite them to share it with your Arts Campers as appropriate!

- *Tuesday: Water*
- *Wednesday: Seeds*
- *Thursday: Soil*

On the Thursday of this camp, Campers gathered at our local urban community garden and we spent the Morning Program and Art session there. Our parish has two plots in the garden, and all produce goes to efforts that feed the hungry. We split the Campers into two small groups: one group did the lesson and then Chalk Art and Nature Art while the other group helped tend the garden, then halfway through the morning we switched activities. We all walked back to the church together, with the Campers divided into groups of about four, with Counselors and Adult Volunteers at the head, middle, and end of the group. Of course we sent information and permission slips home before doing this! (See Sample Letter Home, Appendix 2, p. 111.)

Perhaps your parish keeps a garden, or you have a neighbor whose garden you might use. Or is there an urban farm near you where you could arrange to spend a couple of hours learning and helping? Maybe you have a group of parents who can help transport Campers to and from a garden or farm if walking isn't an option—though make sure your permission form reflects that Campers will be transported by private car, and that no adult is ever in a car with only one child.

Gathering in a garden was a wonderful way to spend the morning. In fact, one of our youngest Campers left fresh produce with the belongings of what was clearly a homeless individual, saying, "Whoever this person is, he is our neighbor too, right?"

- *Friday: Harvest*

The stories we list later in this chapter correspond to the above order of lessons.

Hymns and Songs

In addition to the four listed above in the section on the Morning Program, we suggest the following list of hymns and songs for EcoJustice camp. They are mainly drawn from *The Hymnal 1982* (Church Publishing) and *Lifesongs* (Augsburg Fortress):

- "This is the Day" (#219, *Lift Every Voice and Sing II*)
- "Morning Has Broken" (#8, *The Hymnal 1982*)
- "For the Beauty of the Earth" (We prefer the setting to DIX, by Conrad Kochner, which you can find in *The New Century Hymnal*, # 28)
- "All Things Bright and Beautiful" (#405, *The Hymnal 1982*)
- "The Butterfly Song (#114, *Lifesongs*)
- "Peace Like a River" (#159, *Lifesongs*)
- "We've Got the Whole World in Our Hands" (*Whole World*, Barefoot Books)
- "Arky Arky" (http://www.hymnary.org/hymn/SWM/66)
- "As We Now Go" (http://www.seasonsonline.ca/search/results/inventory/Music-Audio/Download-able-Sheet-Music/As-We-Now-Go) *or* "Alleluia #1" (#178, *The Hymnal 1982*)

ARTS CAMP SUNDAY

Planning

Plan your Arts Camp Sunday Worship with clergy and other parish staff. We recommend that Leaders and Campers present the following portions of the service, which includes incorporating the prepared Offering. Our rector gives us the sermon time for the Arts Camp Offering every year; work with your clergy to decide what is best for your parish.

Here are our recommendations for the service:

Opening Hymn (Campers and Congregation):
- "Morning Has Broken"

Hymn of Praise (in place of the Gloria; Campers call, Congregation responds):
- "This Is the Day"

Sequence Hymn (Campers and Congregation):
- "All Things Bright and Beautiful"

Offertory Anthem (Campers only):
- "The Butterfly Song"

Communion Hymns
- "For the Beauty of the Earth"
- "Peace Like a River"

Closing Hymn
- "As We Now Go" (Campers sing to Congregation first, then all sing together)
- "Alleluia #1"

Postlude
- "Arky Arky" (Use only if, by now, you can still stand it! Our clergy and congregation indulged us this once, but we sang the refrain once at the beginning, then did all of the verses, then sang the refrain twice through—inviting the congregation to join in—at the end. Otherwise this song takes about 10 minutes to sing all the way through!)

Readings

With clergy approval, we recommend the following readings for the Liturgy of the Word during Arts Camp Sunday Worship:

- Old Testament: Genesis 1:1–2:4
- Psalm: Psalm 148
- New Testament: We used the following in place of scripture, with our clergy's blessing; the rector found this piece for us:

A Reading from the Writings of Charles Cummings:

> All creation is a sacrament, a visible sign of the invisible presence. The sacramentality of the creation comes first of all from the fact that the Creator leaves an imprint on every creature, as an artist leaves something of himself or herself in every work. Each fragrant rose or singing bird, every cell or atom, bears some imprint of the divine creative love that brings it into being.
>
> Each individual, essentially related to God by its indelible imprint, exists in the divine presence and mediates the divine presence. This relationship to God gives each being its worth and dignity, its mystery. Because of this relationship, the entire universe and each creature in it can function as a sacrament or sign of God. All creation mediates and expresses something of the mystery of God to those who can read the signs.[4]
>
> Let those with ears to hear, now hear.
>
> *All:* Open our hearts, Most High God.

- Gospel: Matthew 6:25–33

Remember to invite confident older Campers to serve as readers for Sunday. Make sure to give them a copy of the reading and have them practice this part of the liturgy during your Friday rehearsal time. Also make sure the regular Sunday adult readers are not scheduled to read on Arts Camp Sunday.

---

[4]From Charles Cummings, Eco-Spirituality: Toward a Reverent Life (Mahwah, NJ: Paulist Press, 1991). Used with permission.

Eucharistic Prayer 6, from the *Welsh Book of Common Prayer* (http://crucix.com/welsh/communion/cinw-hc-english.pdf, beginning on page 67), is fitting for the Arts Camp Sunday service.

PRE-LUNCHTIME STORIES:

- Monday: *God Created* by Mark Bozzuti-Jones or Genesis 1:1–2:4, *Spark Story Bible* (or the Creation story from any Children's Bible)
- Tuesday: *Song of the Water Boatman & Other Pond Poems* by Joyce Sidman and Beckie Prange
- Wednesday: *The Carrot Seed* by Ruth Krauss and Crockett Johnson
- Thursday: *The Mountain that Loved a Bird* by Alice McLerran and Eric Carle, or *Nature's Green Umbrella* by Gail Gibbons
- Friday: *The Lorax* by Dr. Seuss

Another book to have on hand for a time you may need filler or in case you prefer it to any of the above is *The Barefoot Book of Earth Tales,* which includes stories about our understanding of nature from around the world as well as activities to go with the stories. You may want to add some of their suggestions to our Art projects, or replace any of ours with theirs; you won't hurt our feelings!

GRACE

The Mealtime Blessings in *The Barefoot Book of Blessings* (pp. 18–20) all make mention of the connection between food and the earth.

Two old favorites are also fitting:
> We thank you Lord
> For generous hearts,
> For sun and rainy weather.
> We thank you Lord
> For drink and food,
> And that we are together.
> *Amen.*

> Thank you for the earth so sweet,
> Thank you for the food we eat,
> Thank you for the birds that sing,
> Thank you God for everything!
> *Amen.*

ART

EcoJustice Camp calls for fewer projects than in other Arts Camps because there is one *large* project—each Camper creates and paints a big, beautiful African drum. In addition to the African Drums project, we used a lot of recycled materials and the Campers' personal creativity to make a variety of other art projects throughout the week.

Whole World Drums

Note: We highly recommend you make a drum in advance of camp so the process is familiar and comfortable, and you'll have a finished sample to show the kids.

Concept:

These drums are fun to make and play, and have a central role in the Presentation on Sunday. You'll want each Camper to choose a specific verse from the song *We've Got the Whole World in Our Hands* for the painting on his/her drum, and you want to make sure someone covers each of the verses:

- the whole world
- the sun and the moon
- the mountains and the valleys
- the plains and the deserts
- the lakes and the rivers
- the trees and the flowers
- the birds of the air
- the fish in the sea
- the towns and the cities

Materials:

- cardboard or metal cylinders or hoops (We found industrial-sized cardboard rings, about 18" in diameter and 8" deep, which were wonderful, but you can also use industrial food containers, coffee cans, oatmeal containers, etc. Larger in diameter is better for the kids' artwork. All of the drums do *not* need to be the same size! *Note:* You can buy a set of 4 pre-manufactured drum hoops in a range of sizes [9"–20"] for $10 at: http://www.crazycrow.com/mm5/merchant.mvc?Screen=PROD&-Store_Code=CCTP&Product_Code=6514-2&Category_Code=862-100-000.

- big sheets of paper 3"–4" wider than the diameter of the cylinder or hoop, and heavier than newspaper
- white glue and water
- mixing containers for glue
- scissors
- drawing or scratch paper
- pencils
- acrylic paint (Tempura can be used but will create a weaker drum head.)
- white or off-white acrylic or house paint in larger volume than the other colors
- paint trays or paper plates
- paintbrushes in a variety of sizes, including wide and very fine

Directions:

Monday:

1. Mix equal parts white glue and water in containers.

2. On a big sheet of paper, trace a circle 2" wider than the outside of your cylinder or hoop.

3. Cut out the circle, and cut the leftover paper into strips.

4. Use a wide paintbrush to coat one side of the large cutout circle with the glue mixture.

5. Also coat the side of the cylinder/hoop with the glue mixture. (Once you've painted the glue mixture onto the paper, you need to work gently to avoid tearing. The Campers can do it if they take their time. Senior Counselors should help the youngest children, as well as any Campers whose fine motor skills are limited.)

6. Place the large cutout circle on the face of the cylinder/hoop. This will be the head of the drum.

7. Wrap the edges of the paper around the edges of the cylinder/hoop.

8. Use the brush of your fingers to smooth the paper onto the sides of the cylinder/hoop. Small rips or tears may occur, and can be repaired by placing a paper patch over the tear (on the inside of the drum head if your hoop is open in the back). Simply coat a piece of paper, slightly larger than the tear, with the glue mixture and place it over or under the tear. If a large tear occurs, it is best to start again.

9. Use the paper strips and the glue mixture to wrap the strips of paper around the edges of the drum, securing the edge of the paper head to the sides of the cylinder/hoop.

10. Have a space set aside where the drums can safely sit and dry.

11. In the meantime, make a preliminary drawing for your drum on a plain piece of paper. You can color in the drawing, or simply write down the color you plan to use in each space. Keep your drawing; you'll be working from it all week!

Tuesday:

This is a day to have another project going at the same time as the drums, as there will be drying time between coats of paint. If Campers did not finish their drawings yesterday, they could work on those, then we recommend the Shrink Art project below.

12. Paint the entire face of the drum and the edges of paper that go over onto the sides with white house or acrylic paint. This will serve as a sealer or primer and add strength to the drumhead.

13. Set drums aside to dry, and work on other projects.

14. Before the end of the Art session, your drum should be dry enough to add another coat of paint. Choose a background color (or colors) for the picture you've drawn.

Wednesday:

15. Paint the larger objects from your plan into place. Take time to make the colors vibrant. Do not try to paint smaller details onto these objects until tomorrow

when they've dried. If you don't lay paint on too thickly, it will dry more quickly, and you will likely be able to paint more than one layer in one session.

Thursday:

16. Finish all the small details and finalize your painting.

Friday:

17. Have your finished drum with you for the Arts Camp Sunday Worship rehearsal.

Shrink Art

Concept:

This project reinforces the idea of reusing as much of the packaging that nearly all of our food comes in . . . and is fun! Using the clear plastic from a variety of containers, you'll make ecologically waste-free shrink art.

Materials:

- large, *clear* plastic containers such as take-home boxes from some restaurants and the bins from pre-washed lettuce, spinach, grapes, etc. (*This is often the #5 and #7 plastic that recyclers hate.*)
- permanent markers (*Fine-tipped are best.*)
- hole punchers
- string or thin ribbon or yarn
- toaster ovens (*Gather as many as can be supervised by Volunteers and responsible Senior Counselors.*)
- toaster-oven-size cookie sheets or jelly roll pans (*Note that you will not want to reuse these for cooking after this activity; thrift stores are a great place to find these.*)
- spatulas (*Again, don't plan to reuse for food preparation; these plastics have been connected in some research with a variety of detrimental health effects, especially when heated.*)
- hot pads

Directions:

Note: We *strongly* encourage you to experiment with this activity ahead of time, especially so you see how much the pictures shrink when you bake them.

1. Prepare the plastic containers in advance by cutting large flat pieces; these pieces are what the Campers will use.

2. *Optional:* Print clipart pictures that fit the theme for camp: trees, flowers, animals, the three-arrowed reduce/reuse/recycle symbol, and so on. Kids can place one of these under their clear plastic piece and simply trace and color the picture that way. Of course, many Campers will prefer to create their own pictures, drawings, and more.

3. If the Camper wants the option of hanging their finished creation in a window, or on a necklace or even a keychain, have them poke a hole in the top, not too close to the edge, before baking.

4. An Adult Volunteer or responsible Senior Counselor takes a tray full of finished drawings and places them in a toaster oven preheated to 325°. Watch the drawings constantly, as the process doesn't take long. The plastic will shrink and thicken, hardening in the process, while the Camper's picture miniaturizes.

Notes and Cautions:

- Corners sharpen as the plastic hardens. Be careful!
- Sometimes the plastic in the oven begins to roll up. Push them flat with the spatula before they curl enough to stick to themselves.
- Toasters ovens get *hot!* Make sure Campers know to stay away and that only Adult Volunteers or Counselors are to use them.
- Be aware: this activity is addictive and Campers will make as many shrink art items as you will allow them to make!
- Yes, you can purchase shrinkable plastic sheets at craft stores for this exact activity, but using them negates the "reuse" component of this ecology-based camp.

Crayon Circles

Concept:

This activity shows Campers another creative way to avoid waste and keep waste out of landfills. Together you can clean the broken and too-small crayons out of your Sunday School rooms and replace them with fun, new, circular, multi-colored crayons.

Materials:

- metal muffin or mini-muffin pans
- broken crayons and crayon stubs
- toaster ovens
- hot pads

Directions:

1. Invite Campers to unwrap the old broken crayons and place them together in muffin cups in color combinations they like.

2. An Adult Volunteer or Counselor places the tray in a preheated 300° toaster oven.

3. Watch carefully; it only takes a few minutes for the wax to melt completely.

4. Remove trays from ovens and let the wax cool and harden *completely*, then pop out the new, round, easy-to-hold, multi-colored crayons for use in your classrooms.

Chalk Art and Nature Art

Concept:

Temporary art has a value and ecological message of its own. Campers use chalk—and whatever they find already in place—to create for the sake of creating. This project took place on our Thursday morning at the community garden, and the Campers' imagination and creativity were wondrous to behold. Explain to them in advance that this sort of art, by definition, will be temporary and will be left behind for others to enjoy when you leave the garden. Take photos of their artwork to share on Sunday and also to send home with them after the Sunday service.

Materials:

- sidewalk chalk

Directions:

Note: Fewer instructions for these activities are better than more. Allow for Campers' creativity.

1. Invite Campers to draw with chalk on any concrete or asphalt surface where (a) they are safe and (b) no one will object to their art.

2. Encourage Campers to wander and collect sticks, leaves, grass, rocks, and whatever else they find, then use these items to be creative.

3. Do set some rules with respect to the space you're using: Campers should never remove parts from living, growing plants or trees. Be clear about where they can and cannot go to collect materials, and where they can and can't draw with chalk.

Recycled Creations

Concept:

Creativity meets reuse.

Materials:

For months prior to camp, collect a wide variety of miscellaneous items. We gathered shoeboxes, bottles and tubes and plastic rings, and odd bits of foam from packaging. We had the emptied inner rolls from duct tape and clear tape and packing tape. We saved the strange items from every package we ever opened. The more we looked, the more we found. We did not keep anything made of glass, for safety reasons.

In Denver, there is an amazing non-profit called RAFT (Resource Area For Teaching). It is an artist's dream; a warehouse filled with unwanted or unused random items that people knew better than to throw away; and which are sold for pennies to teachers, including Christian Educators. They have physical stores in Northern California and Denver, as well as an online store at http://www.raft.net. There may be a similar initiative in your area; ask local teachers! If not, inviting the parish to collect and bring in items (rinsed, as appropriate) works as well.

Directions:

On the Friday of camp, once their other projects were finished, we set Campers loose with all of this random stuff. They built in pairs; they built in teams; they built by themselves. Many of them built several projects. Our only rule was that if they built it, they had to be able to take it home at the end of the week!

Tie-Dye

Note: We do this for every year's camp!

Concept:

Our shirts bring us together as a community. Each starts the same, then proclaims how each of us is our own special and unique child of God. No two will ever look alike once they've been dyed! We thank God for camp, for color, for the magic that happens when we combine colors and when we appear to make a mess. We present these shirts to each other, to the congregation, and to God on Sunday when we make our Offering at worship. And we keep the shirts, some of us year after year, to remember the joy, faith, fun, and fellowship of each year's camp.

Materials:

- T-shirts; preordered from a printer (see Chapter 2: *2–4 Weeks before Camp*, p. 18)
- rubber bands for tying shirts
- dye kit including squirt bottles *(Cleaner and safer than vat dyeing!)*
- gallon plastic zipper bags
- paint shirts or trash bag ponchos to cover kids *(optional)*
- non-latex gloves
- tarps
- crates: With 24–28 enrollment, we use two crates.
- large tubs, big enough to hold 2 overturned crates with a bit of room between

Notes:

- We use and highly recommend dyes, fixers, and instructions from Grateful Dyes Inc. They have everything you need plus great instructions, and they ship worldwide. Here is their website: http://www.grateful-dyes.com.
- You can also find tie-dye kits at most hobby stores. Make sure you buy a kit that comes with specific instructions and includes the fixers you need to mix the dyes. You'll want to have everything ready to go when the kids dye their shirts, including three squirt bottles per station with red, yellow, and blue dye. Some kits have you soak shirts in a solution prior to dying; you'll want your Art Instructor(s) and Counselors to make sure this is done ahead of time.
- Instructions and diagrams for dyeing shirts in specific patterns are available from Grateful Dyes as well as all over the Internet!

Directions:

Note: We do this outside on the lawn and still spread tarps . . . this is a messy activity! Putting the tied shirts on an overturned milk crate that in turn is standing in a large metal tray or plastic tub helps catch excess dye. Before you begin, have Senior Counselors mark each shirt with the Campers' initials; you should have compiled a list when you ordered, using the Campers' registration packets to determine each child's size.

1. On Monday, once other art projects are well under way, take small groups and hand out their shirts. Show kids how to twist their shirts and then secure them with rubber bands, helping them as needed.

2. Store the tied shirts in a large tub.

3. On Tuesday and/or Wednesday, have a tie-dye station set up outdoors, close to a door that leads to the art space, if possible. You want at least 1 adult and a counselor for every 4 Campers that are tie-dying.

4. Have Campers put on gloves, and paint shirts or ponchos if desired.

5. Give Campers their tied shirts and have them place them on one of the overturned milk crates in the tub.

6. Using one color at a time, use the squirt bottles to saturate the part of the shirt where you want that color. If you want a very colorful shirt, you need to really soak the area.

7. Repeat step 6 using different colors on the rest of the shirt.

8. Turn the shirt over and repeat steps 6 and 7 on this side. (If children want their shirts to be similar on both sides, have them turn them over as they do each color and section.)

9. Place the finished shirt in a gallon zipper bag and seal it.

10. The Art Instructors will need to rinse the shirts and then run them through a washing machine before they're finished. For a large camp we suggest that the adults all take a batch of shirts home and help out!

11. *Hold onto the shirts until Sunday!* We always show the kids their finished shirts on Friday, but then collect them again to hand out on Sunday morning.

MUSIC

Remember to have poster boards with lyrics[5] for all songs written in advance, and have an Adult Volunteer or Counselor manage and hold them up for the Campers during practices as well as on Sunday.

After warm ups, and in addition to Music games and activities, the daily Music activity is when Campers will learn:

* "The Butterfly Song"
* "Peace Like a River"
* "All Things Bright and Beautiful"
* "Morning Has Broken"

Because they will sing "The Butterfly Song" to the congregation, that should be the main focus of music time. For both "The Butterfly Song" and "Peace Like a River," it can be fun to add movements to the lyrics. If your Campers like that idea, then this is the time to develop and practice those motions. Campers can invent their own motions, although it's also easy to find online the American Sign Language signs for *butterfly, thank, Lord, peace, river,* and so on.

Campers should also practice and be very comfortable with the other two hymns, even though the congregation will be joining to sing them.

MOVEMENT/DRAMA

This is where Campers will learn the song "We've Got the Whole World in Our Hands," as well as create an original script to go along with the lyrics of the song. The Movement/Drama Instructor shares the book, *Whole World,* with the group. The book is small, but the illustrations are rich, so reading it in smaller groups is ideal. The added material in the back of the book can be shared at the first reading or saved for the next day.

Informally sing the song through once, to make sure all the kids are familiar with the tune and timing. Then explain that for Sunday's Offering, Campers will have a chance to teach the congregation about ecology and stewardship of God's creation. So, during the next couple of days, they'll be working together to create that Offering.

Here's an outline for how that will work:

1. To begin the Offering, Campers line up at the front of the sanctuary, staggered on the step(s) (if you have them) so that each Camper has space to hold his or her Whole World Drum up, with the painted face showing, and wave it gently back and forth, and so that everyone in the congregation can see some, if not all, of the children. With a large camp, have Campers stand in the aisles as well!

2. All Campers sing:

   We've got the whole world in our hands,
   We've got the whole world in our hands,
   We've got the whole world in our hands,
   We've got the whole world in our hands!

3. Pause between each of the verses; during each pause, a small group of Campers will speak. See below for more details.

4. For the rest of the verses, all Campers sing, while those who painted the images specific to the verse raise their drums and sway them gently to and fro in time to the music:

   She's got the sun and the moon in her hands . . .

   He's got the mountains and the valleys in his hands . . .

   She's got the plains and the deserts in her hands . . .

---

[5] Save your poster boards, as you never know when you might want to reuse one and there are some songs you'll use every year. We do this for our Christmas pageant hymns, as well.

He's got the lakes and the rivers in his hands . . .

She's got the trees and the flowers in her hands . . .

He's got the birds of the air in his hands . . .

She's got the fish of the sea in her hands . . .

He's got the towns and the cities in his hands . . .

5. For the final verse, invite the congregation to join you in singing "We've got the whole world in our hands . . ." as all Campers raise their drums and wave them. If you have a group that can do it, pass the drums in a pattern amongst one another during this verse, on the beat. Make sure you have the rows passing different directions, so the drums go back the other way once they've reached the end of the line!

We've got the whole world in our hands . . .

6. *And for the lines that occur between verses:* Throughout the week during Drama, guide Campers to identify the piece of information they want to share during Sunday's Offering. Write these down on index cards (or invite Campers to do so). Our Campers enjoyed sharing environmental and ecological facts as well as suggestions about ways to help save the planet. The cards can then be secured to the inside rim of the child's drum using blue painter's tape (to avoid damage to the drum).

These observations and comments are shared between verses of the song. Space the Campers' readings so that everyone has one turn and they are evenly spaced between the verses. There are nine spaces to fill, so, for example if you have 27 Campers, you'll want to have three of them read between each verse. As you see, you can accommodate a large camp by placing four or five readers between each verse. With a very large group, kids could team up in pairs to come up with their lines and read them together at their turn.

This Offering is logistically simple, since all the kids will need are their drums with their index cards taped inside. They'll be wearing their tie-dye shirts, and it is a beautiful and colorful offering to God and the congregation.

POPSICLES/SNACK, GAMES, AND CLOSING THE CAMP DAY

See Chapter 6 (p. 35) for specifics on ending the day and Appendix 3 (p. 117) for tried-and-true camp games.

FRIDAY AFTERNOON

Before you pray and sing, which should be the last act of the last day of Arts Camp, you may want to leave time for an evaluation. A simple evaluation form can be found in Appendix 2 (p. 114).

You'll also want to make sure Campers take home the things they brought with them at the beginning of the week and that have accumulated throughout camp: water bottles, beach towels, sweaters and sweatshirts, hats and sunglasses. Also send home any art projects that you do *not* want to use or display on Sunday. Keep tie-dye shirts and everything else they will wear or display on Sunday.

You'll want your Art Instructor(s) and Counselors to spend time following the last Art session on Friday setting up a display of the Campers' creations so that is in place for Sunday.

Finally, send a note home with each family on Friday afternoon thanking them for bringing their children to camp and giving them details on the Sunday service, including what time Campers should arrive. You want time for Campers to put on their tie-dye shirts and to come to the choir loft to practice before the service begins. A sample of this note home can be found with the forms in Appendix 2 (p. 113). We copy this note on brightly colored paper and place it next to the sign-out sheet for parents to see and take when they come to pick up their Campers.

As with every day of Arts Camp, but especially on Friday, you'll want your Counselors to stay later so they can help you put camp away!

Throughout the week, we have parents who tend to arrive to pick up their children a little early, so they've seen and heard our closing prayer and song. On Friday, once we've given instructions for taking things home and final cleanup, invite parents and caregivers to join the circle at this time. Then try not to get emotional as you sing your goodbye blessing and realize that Arts Camp is over for the year.

CHAPTER 9

Arts Camp: Who Is My Neighbor?

You shall love the Lord your God with all your heart, and with all your soul, and with all your mind. This is the greatest and first commandment. And the second is like it: You shall love your neighbor as yourself. —Matthew 22:37–39

 HE COMMAND TO LOVE OUR NEIGHBOR AS ourselves is so clear, so seemingly simple, yet we struggle as a society to truly live into this aspect of God's kingdom. This camp starts on Monday with a study of the self, then builds outward to establish who, indeed, *are* the neighbors Jesus calls us to love unconditionally. Elementary school children are concrete thinkers, so when we tell them to love their neighbors, they will envision the actual people in the houses and apartments near their own. They may have learned in Sunday School that in outreach we extend our hand to more distant neighbors—the people on the prayer list, the poor and hungry, and so forth. This Arts Camp helps Campers broaden their definition to fit Christ's true call to us—to love everyone as an extension of our love for the Lord our God.

MORNING PROGRAM

Remember to have the sign-in/sign-out sheet ready for parents and caregivers, and nametags and markers for all Campers for the morning check-in time.

Also have scripture passages and quotes printed on card stock and either hanging up or ready to hang up once you've used them in your Morning Program.

Always call Campers together in the mornings with a song. "This Is the Day" is wonderful for gathering the children in the morning, and "Hallelujah! Praise ye the Lord!" works beautifully for transitions, including ending the Morning Program and heading off to Art, Music, and Drama (see Chapter 3, p. 23).

Introduce yourself and do an introduction activity (we offer one, Who Are We? found in Appendix 3, p. 121), then say a prayer for your day together:

May we be filled with loving-kindness.
May we be well.
May we be peaceful and at ease.
May we be happy.

- *Monday:*
Begin by reading Genesis 1 from any good children's Bible. We used Desmond Tutu's *Children of God Storybook Bible,* which is lovely. Focus particularly on the words "So God created human kind in God's image." Discuss this idea with the Campers:
  — If we are each created in God's image, what does that tell us about God's love for us? about judging people because of their color? their size? their gender? other?

Next read Psalm 139:1, 13–18. Ask Campers to close their eyes and listen carefully to the words and to the way they sound like a song. Say:
  — If there are words you don't know, let them breeze over you and don't stop to worry about them.
  — See if you can hear what God is telling us about ourselves and each other.

Read the psalm, post it on the wall behind you if you haven't already, and then ask the kids questions about what they heard. Emphasize the idea of God's knowing each one of us, intimately, even before we are born.

- *Tuesday:*
Today we branch our exploration from the self to those closest to us—our family and friends. The reading is Luke 5:17–26, the story of the paralytic man whose friends lower him through the roof to get to Jesus. Now that's friendship!

Ask questions for brief discussion:
— Who are the people in your family? Share this with the person to your right.
— Who here has a really good friend?
— Can brothers and sisters be friends?
— Can you have too many friends?
— Have you made a new friend at camp? *or* Would you like to make a friend today?

Conduct a quick activity:
1. Ask everyone who has a cat *(or dog, or brother, or bicycle, etc.)* to stand up.
2. Have the standing kids spread apart from one another.
3. Tell those who are seated to stand up and go to someone who is standing, learn that Camper's name, and learn one other important thing about that person *(the cat's name, the brother's age, the color of the bike, etc.)*.
4. Repeat with different initial questions as time allows, with the rule that the children must find a new partner each time. Other questions could be: Who is going into second grade? Who loves to sing? Who is wearing flip–flops?

- *Wednesday:*
We've talked about ourselves as being created in God's image, and we've talked about family and friends. Now we branch to an exploration of our "neighbor." Once you've sung your opening song and prayed, read or tell the story of the Good Samaritan to the children. A wonderful rendering of this story is in Desmond Tutu's *Children of God Storybook Bible,* but

of course you can use any version you prefer or have available.

Once Campers have heard the story, ask questions and lead a discussion. You may want to help the Campers understand that Samaritans were considered outsiders and undesirables to the people of Jesus' time and place. *Possible questions:*
— Was the injured traveler the Samaritan's actual neighbor?
— Why did the other travelers pass by the man who had been robbed and beaten?
— Why did the Samaritan stop?
— How can we be good Samaritans in our time and place? *(This is a question we'll be exploring during drama all week, as well.)*

- *Thursday:*
Gather outdoors if that's possible—even return to the community or parish garden, if you are able (see Chapter 8). Sing and pray, then talk about food, gardens, urban farming, organic food, and sustainable farming. Help children understand how buying local food helps our community and our faraway neighbors as well.

Read Matthew 25:35–40 to the children. Then lead a discussion about food justice and the fact that while some of us have plenty to eat—sometimes so much that we end up throwing food away when we're full!—we have neighbors both near and far who are chronically hungry. Talk about ministries of your parish and community that help give healthy food to hungry people.

- *Friday:*
Review with the children what they've learned or discovered about what it means to be a good neighbor. You could discuss:
— Who are our neighbors, in terms of God's plan for all of us?
— How can we extend these ideas to our planet, our "global village"?

Use Friday morning to clarify all of the learning from the week and to fill in any blanks that have been left empty.

Hymns and Songs

- "This is the Day" (#219, *Lift Every Voice and Sing II*)
- "Hallelujah! Praise ye the Lord!" (#179, *Lifesongs*)
- "Arky Arky" (http://www.hymnary.org/hymn/SWM/66)
- "I'm Gonna Sing" (#117, *Lift Every Voice and Sing II*)
- "All Are Welcome" (http://www.giamusic.com/search_details.cfm?title_id=209)
- "Who Is My Neighbor?" (Sheet music available in Appendix 1, p. 99.)
- "Will You Come and Follow Me" (#757, *Wonder Love and Praise*)
- "The Servant Song" (#94, *My Heart Sings Out*; #539, *The New Century Hymnal*)
- "Jesu, Jesu, Fill Us with Your Love" (#602, *The Hymnal 1982*)
- "As We Now Go" (http://www.seasonsonline.ca/search/results/inventory/Music-Audio/Download-able-Sheet-Music/As-We-Now-Go) or
- "Alleluia No. 1" (#178, *The Hymnal 1982*)

ARTS CAMP SUNDAY

Planning

Plan your Arts Camp Sunday Worship service with clergy and other parish staff. We recommend that Leaders and Campers present the following portions of the service, which includes incorporating the prepared Offering. Our rector gives us the sermon time for the Arts Camp Offering every year; work with your clergy to decide what is best for your parish.

Here are our recommendations for the service:

Entrance Hymn (Campers and Congregation)
- "All Are Welcome"
- *Hymn of Praise* (In place of the Gloria, Campers and Congregation)
- "Hallelujah, Praise ye the Lord!"

Sequence Hymn
- "Who Is My Neighbor?" (Campers Only)

- "Will You Come and Follow Me?" (Campers and Congregation)

Offertory Anthem
- "The Servant Song" (with hand bells)

Communion Hymn
- "Jesu, Jesu, Fill Us with Your Love"

Closing Hymn
- "As We Now Go"
- "Alleluia No. 1"

Readings

With clergy approval, we recommend the following readings for the Liturgy of the Word during Arts Camp Sunday Worship:
- Old Testament: Jeremiah 31:7–9
- Psalm: Psalm 139:13–16
- New Testament: Acts 4:32–37
- Gospel: Matthew 25:31–40

Remember to invite confident older Campers to serve as readers for Sunday. Make sure to give them a copy of the reading and have them practice this part of the liturgy during your Friday rehearsal time. Also make sure adult parishioners are not scheduled to read on Arts Camp Sunday.

Eucharistic Prayer 6, from the *Welsh Book of Common Prayer* (http://crucix.com/welsh/communion/cinw-hc-english.pdf, beginning on p. 67), is fitting for the Arts Camp Sunday service.

PRE-LUNCHTIME STORIES

- Monday: *Me!* by Philip Waechter
- Tuesday: "Joseph Is Sold into Slavery" and "Joseph Feeds and Forgives," *Children of God Storybook Bible* by Archbishop Desmond Tutu
- Wednesday: *God in Between* by Sandy Eisenberg Sasso and Sally Sweetland
- Thursday: "Jesus Blesses the Little Children," *Children of God Storybook Bible* by Archbishop Desmond Tutu
- Friday: *Yertle the Turtle* by Dr. Seuss

GRACE

See Chapter 5, page 33 for a variety of resources.

ART

Art projects this week follow the expanding theme of looking at ourselves, then our friends and family, then our community, nation, and world all as "neighbors."

Me, Myself, and I

Concept:
The scripture reading from this morning tells us that we are, each of us, created in God's image. Take a closer look at how our Creator is presented in each person present!

Materials:
- large butcher paper, cut in 5'–6' lengths
- pencils
- markers or paint
- scissors
- plenty of floor space

Directions:
1. Have Campers pair up—younger children paired with Junior Counselors is a great idea for this project.

2. Give each Camper a piece of butcher paper. Each piece of paper needs to be a bit taller than the Camper.

3. One Camper lays down on his/her piece of butcher paper in any position. Some of our Campers chose to look like they were flying, in mid-leap, or other joy-filled poses.

4. The Camper holds still while the other in the pair traces all the way around, taking time and care to make a clear representation of the first Camper's shape.

5. Trade places and repeat steps 1–4 with the partner Camper.

6. Next, Campers cut their silhouette out, as close to the line as possible.

7. Campers begin the process of filling in their silhouettes with color and detail.

Encourage Campers to create themselves in clothing that fits their personality well, and with accurate skin colors and facial expressions. Both Junior and Senior Counselors can be available to help the younger Campers . . . or anyone who struggles with drawing details.

Chain of Love and Friendship

Concept:
Remember paper dolls and the magic of unfolding them and seeing all their clasped hands? Most modern children have never had that experience, and this is a perfect theme to introduce it to them.

Note: For a video that clearly shows how to make paper dolls, the Internet is a lovely source: http://www.youtube.com/watch?v=MeTh8AjxmPc.

Materials:
- camera or smartphone camera
- construction paper
- markers or crayons
- scissors

Directions:
1. *On Monday,* take a snapshot of each Camper. They can pose or not pose, but do try to get them looking happy and genuine. Either print these photos on a personal photo printer *or* send them out to a one-hour photo developer so you'll have them by Tuesday (or even Wednesday is okay).

2. Fold a long piece of construction paper in half lengthwise once, twice, and then a third time. Always fold from the left edge to the right.

3. Draw half of a person on the top layer of paper, starting at the left edge and making sure the figure's hand extends to the right edge of the paper. This is where the paper-doll chain will connect.

4. Cut along the line you drew.

5. Campers should make one or two chains with enough dolls to represent their family members and their closest friends.

6. Color each of the individual dolls to represent a family member or close friend. Do not color one for yourself.

7. Give the children their snapshots, and have them tape the back of their photo to the backs of the hands of whichever two friends or family members they want to stand between in their chain of love.

Mobile

Concept:

This is a more abstract project; let your Art Instructor decide whether to use it and how to tweak it to make sense for your camp. With a talented Art Instructor who is great at collecting a variety of seemingly random items and putting them together to make art, it worked very well for our camp.

Never underestimate the innate creativity of children; given time, a variety of materials, and *less* instruction, they will amaze you with their invention and imagination!

As you widen your explorations this week from the self to family and friends to the wider community, encourage Campers to create a mobile that reflects this outward expansion. This means incorporating into each mobile an item that represents the self, another item for family, yet another for friends, then school/church/community, then nation, then world.

This project could be scheduled in two ways: (1) Have Campers make the hanger on Monday, along with their item for self. Then make an additional item each day as you expand the perspective. (2) Make the whole thing on Thursday and Friday.

Materials:

- 1'–2' sticks or dowels
- wide variety of art materials: various sizes of card stock, lids from butter tubs, metal ends of frozen juice concentrate, yarn, fabric scraps, craft sticks, foam letters and symbols, etc. (*Dollar and craft stores typically offer a wonderful variety of small items that kids could use or make, and using natural and recycled items is a nice way to remind ourselves about stewardship.*)
- white glue
- scissors
- yarn, twine, and/or strong kitchen string
- *Optional:* a hot glue gun and designated Adult Volunteers and Counselors to help Campers use it

Directions:

Truly, this is a time to give kids fewer instead of more directions; here's what you need to get started:

1. Campers can decide whether to make a mobile from one stick or small branch, or from two that are crossed in the middle.

2. For Campers who want two crossed sticks, an Adult Volunteer or Counselor should help hold the sticks together and secure them by tying a piece of twine or string firmly around one stick. Leave about 8"–12" of twine or string loose before you tie it: this will serve as a way to hang the mobile.

3. Wrap the twine or string repeatedly, in a crisscrossing pattern, around the place where the sticks cross until they stay in place.

4. Leave another 8"–12" length of string or twine when you cut so you'll have enough to hang the mobile from a variety of places.

5. Have Campers make the items they want on their mobiles, then tie them from the mobile. It looks best if you hang each item at a slightly different length.

Beads

Concept:

Campers make beads with the intent of trading them on Friday as a gesture of friendship.

Materials:

- sculpting clay such as Model Magic® and/or Play Doh® in a variety of colors
- chopsticks
- yarn
- large trays, or a designated table covered with plastic, to place beads while they dry
- wax paper
- permanent marker or crayons

Directions:

1. Set a strip of wax paper on the trays or table where you will have Campers set their beads to dry.

2. Use the clay to make beads in a variety of shapes and sizes. You want them to be big enough to poke a hole through for stringing, but not too big to string and wear on a necklace.

3. Once you've made each bead, use a chopstick to poke a hole through the middle.

4. Lay your beads—close together but without touching—on a section of waxed paper, and then mark your section using a permanent marker or crayon and write your name inside it.

5. It's important to tell Campers that while they're welcome to make one or two beads for themselves, they will be giving as many beads as possible away to camp friends on Friday, and receiving beads from friends as well. We like to give the directions for this project early in the week, so Campers can make beads whenever they have free time. Be sure to make

beads by Wednesday at the latest so they'll be hardened before kids trade and string them on Friday.

6. Leave time on Friday for Campers to trade beads, then use yarn or string to make themselves a necklace of their beads. Have them wrap their necklace inside their tie-dyed shirt so they can wear both on Sunday.

Props for Drama

As your Campers develop one-act plays in Drama this week, they may find a need for some small props. If possible, these can be made during Art sessions throughout the week. This is a great task for Counselors or any Campers who are quick finishers. See the Drama section on page 67.

Tie-Dye

Note: We do this for every year's camp!

Concept:

Our shirts bring us together as a community. Each starts the same, then proclaims how each of us is our own special and unique child of God. No two will ever look alike once they've been dyed! We thank God for camp, for color, for the magic that happens when we combine colors and when we appear to make a mess. We present these shirts to each other, to the congregation, and to God on Sunday when we make our Offering at worship. And we keep the shirts, some of us year after year, to remember the joy, faith, fun, and fellowship of each year's camp.

Materials:

- T-shirts; preordered from a printer (see Chapter 2: *2–4 Weeks before Camp*, p. 18)
- rubber bands for tying shirts
- dye kit including squirt bottles *(Cleaner and safer than vat dyeing!)*
- gallon plastic zipper bags
- paint shirts or trash bag ponchos to cover kids *(optional)*
- non-latex gloves
- tarps

- crates: With 24–28 enrollment, we use two crates.
- large tubs, big enough to hold 2 overturned crates with a bit of room between

Notes:

- We use and highly recommend dyes, fixers, and instructions from Grateful Dyes Inc. They have everything you need plus great instructions, and they ship worldwide. Here is their website: http://www.grateful-dyes.com.
- You can also find tie-dye kits at most hobby stores. Make sure you buy a kit that comes with specific instructions and includes the fixers you need to mix the dyes. You'll want to have everything ready to go when the kids dye their shirts, including three squirt bottles per station with red, yellow, and blue dye. Some kits have you soak shirts in a solution prior to dying; you'll want your Art Instructor(s) and Counselors to make sure this is done ahead of time.
- Instructions and diagrams for dyeing shirts in specific patterns are available from Grateful Dyes as well as all over the Internet!

Directions:

Note: We do this outside on the lawn and still spread tarps . . . this is a messy activity! Putting the tied shirts on an overturned milk crate that in turn is standing in a large metal tray or plastic tub helps catch excess dye. Before you begin, have Senior Counselors mark each shirt with the Campers' initials; you should have compiled a list when you ordered, using the Campers' registration packets to determine each child's size.

1. On Monday, once other art projects are well under way, take small groups and hand out their shirts. Show kids how to twist their shirts and then secure them with rubber bands, helping them as needed.
2. Store the tied shirts in a large tub.
3. On Tuesday and/or Wednesday, have a tie-dye station set up outdoors, close to a door that leads to the Art space, if possible. You want at least one adult and a Counselor for every four Campers who are tie-dying.
4. Have Campers put on gloves and paint shirts/ponchos, if desired.
5. Give Campers their tied shirts and have them place them on of the overturned milk crates in the tub.
6. Using one color at a time, use the squirt bottles to saturate the part of the shirt where you want that color. If you want a very colorful shirt, you need to really soak the area.
7. Repeat step 6 using different colors on the rest of the shirt.
8. Turn the shirt over and repeat steps 6 and 7 on this side. (If children want their shirts to be similar on both sides, have them turn them over as they do each color and section.)
9. Place the finished shirt in a gallon zipper bag and seal it.
10. The Art Instructors will need to rinse the shirts and then run them through a washing machine before they're finished. For a large camp we suggest that the adults all take a batch of shirts home and help out!
11. *Hold onto the shirts until Sunday!* We always show the kids their finished shirts on Friday, but then collect them again to hand out on Sunday morning.

MUSIC

As always, it is our plan that you sing "This is the Day" and "Hallelujah! Praise ye the Lord!" during your Morning Program and "As We Now Go" (or another closing song) at the close of each day's camp.

The main learning for Music sessions this week will be "The Servant Song" with a simple hand-bell arrangement, and "Who Is My Neighbor" if you choose to use it. You can buy sheet music for "The Servant Song" at http://www.hymnary.org, though many parishes already own an arrangement; check with your Music Instructor. The sheet music for "Who Is My Neighbor," which was written for the children and youth of St. Barnabas, is in Appendix 1 and is yours to use with the purchase of this book. You do not need to buy sheet music for Campers.

Instead, give them each a copy of the lyrics, highlighted so that they play their bell as they sing a word or syllable. Children can learn to sing the song while they play, without having to read music, and it makes timing the bells easier.

Clearly, much of your music time this week will be exploring with hand bells; learning how to hold them, ring them, and tamp them, and then learning to actually sing and play the song. Remember to keep it fun and have music-oriented games and activities to begin and end each session as well.

About hand bells:

- If your parish does not own bells, ask other local churches or schools if they have a set you could borrow or rent for the week.
- Otherwise, there are small bell sets geared to kids available on the Internet for much less money than a regular set. While they won't have the same range or tone, some of them work quite well. We believe that a decent set of hand bells is a great investment for any children's ministry.
- Hand bells should always be held and played in gloved hands. Plan ahead; in the winter you can buy inexpensive children's cotton gloves for $1 a pair (check the dollar store!). You could also ask parishioners to donate new or gently used cotton gloves.

MOVEMENT/DRAMA

For Sunday's Offering during the Arts Camp Sunday service, Campers work together to create original one-act plays that illustrate real-life Good Samaritan scenarios in our modern world. After a warm-up activity, your Movement/Drama Instructor needs to begin on Monday by having kids name times in their lives they've seen someone in need. Try for a wide variety—homeless people on the street corners, a child being picked on at school, a neighbor in some need or distress. Generally, we find that once Campers know what we're looking for, they are able to name many instances of witnessing

people whose needs are not being met. Often, they see what we miss.

Form groups as naturally as possible; you want each group to have approximately the same number of Campers and each group to have a Counselor or Adult Volunteer to guide them. If numbers won't allow that, try to place your most capable Junior Counselors or older Campers in any group that doesn't have a Senior Counselor or Adult Volunteer.

Give each group a clipboard with plain, lined paper. Assign an older Camper to be the scribe. Groups don't necessarily have to write a full script; what they need is a list of the characters they'll be portraying and a general outline of what will happen in their scenario. Have them spend more time actually creating a dramatization than they do writing anything down.

You need to know ahead of time how many groups you'll use and how many minutes each group has to present their scene. This will be dependent on the number of Campers and how much time you've been given for the Sunday Offering. We are given the sermon time each year, and because our service is always a bit shorter than the average, we take 15–18 minutes for our Offering. In this case, if we have five or six groups, we keep the time for each to about 3 minutes. This may seem short, but it is enough if you guide the Campers in how to keep their dramatization succinct. They don't want to spend time on anything but the clear story; this will be a good lesson in dramatic performance for them.

Of course you will have a mix of Campers who were born to be on stage, those who would rather eat nothing but lima beans for the rest of their lives, and a large number who fall in the middle. Encourage each group to meet the needs of each individual member as they assign and work up their roles.

These dramas will necessarily evolve throughout the week. On Wednesday tell Campers that it is their last chance to make any big changes. Thursday they should be able to practice and then present their scenes to each other, offering gentle feedback about understanding and clarity. By Friday they should be able to rehearse their scenes fairly smoothly as part of your preparation for the Arts Camp Sunday Worship.

Note: We had a group that wanted to act out a bullying situation one of the Campers had witnessed at school, which involved one child hitting another. We taught them how to do a staged hit safely and carefully, made sure they understood the importance of keeping it controlled, and let parents know in advance that this would be happening. It worked, and the congregation was moved at the powerful demonstration of what even our elementary-aged children experience in their school days. We did have a small brother who, too young to understand, was upset at seeing his big brother "hit." This was quickly solved by having big brother go sit with the little one as soon as possible afterwards and showing him there was "no owie."

POPSICLES/SNACK, GAMES, AND CLOSING THE CAMP DAY

See Chapter 6 (p. 35) for specifics on ending the day and Appendix 3 (p. 117) for tried-and-true camp games.

FRIDAY AFTERNOON

Before you pray and sing, which should be the last act of the last day of Arts Camp, you may want to leave time for an evaluation. A simple evaluation form can be found in Appendix 2 (p. 114).

You'll also want to make sure Campers take home the things they brought with them at the beginning of the week and that have accumulated throughout camp: water bottles, beach towels, sweaters and sweatshirts, hats and sunglasses. Also send home any art projects that you do *not* want to use or display on Sunday. Keep tie-dye shirts and everything else they will wear or display on Sunday.

You'll want your Art Instructor(s) and Counselors to spend time following the last Art session on Friday

setting up a display of the Campers' creations so that is in place for Sunday.

Finally, send a note home with each family on Friday afternoon thanking them for bringing their children to camp and giving them details on the Sunday service, including what time Campers should arrive. You want time for Campers to put on their tie-dye shirts and to come to the choir loft to practice before the service begins. A sample of this note home can be found with the forms in Appendix 2 (p. 113). We copy this note on brightly colored paper and place it next to the sign-out sheet for parents to see and take when they come to pick up their Campers.

As with every day of Arts Camp, but especially on Friday, you'll want your Counselors to stay later so they can help you put camp away!

Throughout the week, we have parents who tend to arrive to pick up their children a little early, so they've seen and heard our closing prayer and song. On Friday, once we've given instructions for taking things home and final cleanup, invite parents and caregivers to join the circle at this time. Then try not to get emotional as you sing your goodbye blessing and realize that Arts Camp is over for the year.

CHAPTER 10

Arts Camp: Interfaith Peace

What does it mean to be a Christian?

What other faith traditions are there?

How are other faith traditions similar to Christianity?

How can learning about each other's faith help us become peacemakers?

 HIS IS POSSIBLY OUR FAVORITE ARTS CAMP ever. Kids and adults alike walked away from this week feeling open, accepting and accepted, and so much more knowledgeable about how truly connected we *all* are. The Sunday Offering was eye-opening for our congregation, which, despite its progressive demographic, still had a lot to learn about the many ways other faiths are not so different from our own. While we've incorporated meditation into the Arts Camp schedule throughout this book, this was the year we actually started it and, like Frost's less-traveled path, it has made all the difference!

Please note, this Arts Camp is all about diversity, inclusion, unity, and acceptance of differences. It focuses on the peaceful spiritual practices of Christians, Muslims, Jews, Native Americans, Buddhists, and Hindi. Our conversations acknowledged the many ways and times religion has historically been used to divide and discriminate. This camp challenges oft-accepted stereotypes and focuses on understanding as a path to peace.

Cultural sensitivity for this camp means learning about and exploring others' worship, prayer, music, and ceremony traditions in a spirit of education and acceptance. It is not disrespectful to "try on" another culture's practices when we do so in this spirit. It becomes disrespectful only when there is a sense of "making fun." Emphasize from the beginning that the goal of the week is to learn about and understand others, and that sometimes you'll try out their traditions to see how they feel and compare them to our own experiences.

MORNING PROGRAM

Remember to have the sign-in/sign-out sheet ready for parents and caregivers, and nametags and markers for all Campers for the morning check-in time.

Also have scripture passages and quotes printed on card stock and either hanging up or ready to be hung up once you've used them in your morning sessions.

Always call camp together in the mornings with a song. As before, "This Is the Day" is wonderful for gathering the children in the morning, and "Hallelujah! Praise ye the Lord!" works beautifully for transitions, including ending the Morning Program and heading off to Art, Music, and Drama sessions (see Chapter 3).

Introduce yourself and do an introduction activity (we offer one, Who Are We? found in Appendix 3, p. 121), then say a prayer for your day together:

May we be filled with loving-kindness.
May we be well.
May we be peaceful and at ease.
May we be happy.

We used the World Peace Village for our programming for this camp, and recommend it highly: http://www. worldpeacevillage.org. For $35 (plus $16 for a great

CD) you can buy their "Table Top World Peace Village." (They sell through the Reach and Teach Store online. When you click on the order tab, you will be taken to that site.) Combined with the resources and information about each of six world religions on the World Peace Village website, this kit provided us with most of what we needed and used for our Morning Programs. All we added were some favorite quotes of peacemakers past and present, which we used to fill time and add thought-provoking décor on the wall behind our circle area.

We also purchased *The Kids Book of World Religions* by Jennifer Glossop and John Mantha and *One World Many Religions: The Ways We Worship* by Mary Pope Osborne. Both offered excellent supplementary material for Camp, including illustrations and photographs. I kept these books out in our central area throughout the week for any moment we had a question that wasn't answered elsewhere, or when we needed pictures to aid understanding.

World Peace Village includes the following faith traditions (also included are the days of the week to explore each):

- All Week: Christianity, as it relates to the remaining five . . .
- Monday: Islam
- Tuesday: Judaism
- Wednesday: Native American Spirituality
- Thursday: Buddhism
- Friday: Hinduism

We explored the latter five through the lens of our Christian faith, focusing on the ways our faiths are connected.

World Peace Village includes a list of sacred items for each religious tradition. We asked local temples and mosques to help us by loaning us examples of worship items. They were gracious, kind, and excited to know that we planned to teach about their faith traditions respectfully. Each day, as we learned about a new religion, we investigated the sacred items we'd borrowed. If you can't find the items you'd like, print photos of them from an Internet search so you'll have them to show the children.

Prepare card stock with each faith's Peace Prayer, Peace Greeting, Peace Words, and Golden Rule, all of which are available on World Peace Village's website, included in the tabletop kit, and through a myriad of other Internet searches. You might place Christianity in the center, as a way to highlight how our own faith experience fits with the ones you'll be exploring all week. Additional ideas for quotes you might like to display and use this week include:

- Out beyond ideas of wrongdoing and right doing there is a field; I will meet you there. (Rumi)
- And still, after all this time, the sun has never said to the earth, "You owe me." Look what happens with love like that; It lights up the world. (Hafez)
- Do not use Buddhism to become Buddhist . . . use it to become better at whatever else in your life you are doing already. (The Dalai Lama)
- The highest form of wisdom is kindness. (The Talmud)
- Peace starts first with you; then it becomes contagious. (John Roger)
- Understanding and love are not two things; just one. (Thich Nhat Hanh)
- Only a sane spiritual rebuilding of the human race can bring about peace. To set about the task, we must go back to the child. (Maria Montessori)
- Character is how you treat those who can do nothing for you. (Johann Von Goethe)
- When I admire the wonders of a sunset or the beauty of the moon, my soul expands in the worship of the Creator. (Mahatma Gandhi)
- In a gentle way, you can shake the world. (Mahatma Gandhi)
- Prayer is not asking. It is a longing of the soul. It is daily admission of one's weakness. It is better in prayer to have a heart without words than words without a heart. (Mahatma Gandhi)

You can find many additional quotes to fit your ideas and goals online, of course.

At the very beginning of Arts Camp, on Monday morning, pull your gathering together with the words, "Peace be with you!" or "May the peace of the Lord be always with you!" Your response will depend on the Campers' familiarity with these words. Like many parishes, we tend to use them to get attention at every gathering, so our hall rang with "And also with you!"

Next review the Golden Rule ("Do unto others as you would have them do unto you.") and ask wondering questions about what this means and how we do and do not use it in our everyday lives.

Finally, read St. Francis' prayer, "Make Me an Instrument of Thy Peace," which you will use as the Christian peace prayer all week. With the Christian Peace Words, Golden Rule, and Peace Prayer in place, you'll move on to the other two Abrahamic faiths and then the other three religious explorations.

Each day, start by asking Campers what they already know about the religion you're focusing on that day. Check for stereotypes and labels. For instance, Campers may have learned that Islam is a violent religion, which is patently untrue even though it, like other religions, has been misused and misunderstood by both its own followers and those outside its tradition. Older Campers may already know that historically, religion and religious differences have been a common cause for violence, exclusion, and war. Interfaith Arts Camp is about finding the ties that bind us together. So you will learn the peace greeting and its response and repeat them to each other throughout the day. Read the Peace Prayer and Peace Words together, inviting children to note the similarities between the various traditions' versions.

Each day, teach the Campers the peace greeting for that day's faith tradition. So, on Monday, you'll say *"Asa-laam Alaikum!"* (You can find help with pronunciation by reaching out to a local mosque or through an online search.) Teach them the response: *"Alaikum Asalaam!"* This is the Muslim and Arabic version of "Peace be with you," and "And also with you!" Every time you need the Campers' attention, use the peace greeting and response for that day.

You might like to tell or read the story of Abraham on Monday morning, as a reminder that the God of Abraham is the God of Christians and is also the God of Muslims. Tuesday, you'll introduce Judaism as the third Abrahamic faith.

Many spiritual traditions have feasts and holy days. Ramadan is an important religious observation for Muslim people, and is similar to Lent in many ways: fasting, prayer, and a refocusing on God's will in our lives. Rosh Hashanah and Yom Kippur are high holy days for Jews that are less known to many Christian children than Hanukkah. Information for holy days, celebrations, feasts, and practices can be found on the World Peace Village website as well as through an Internet search. For best success, focus on celebrations with which you feel you can best connect yourself and your Campers.

Hymns and Songs

- "This Is the Day" (#219, *Lift Every Voice and Sing II*)
- "Hallelujah! Praise ye the Lord!" (#179, *Lifesongs*)
- "Arky Arky" (http://www.hymnary.org/hymn/SWM/66)
- "I'm Gonna Sing" (# 117, *Lift Every Voice and Sing II*)
- "Peace Mandala" (see section on Music in this chapter)
- "Now I Walk in Beauty" (traditional Navajo prayer, sung in a round: https://www.youtube.com/watch?v=EOhZujNbYg8)
- "Let There Be Peace on Earth" (http://www.music-notes.com/landing?w=Let+There+Be+Peace+on+Earth)
- "Prayer of Peace" (http://www.hymnary.org/text/peace_before_us_peace_behind_us)
- "Shalom Chaverim" (#107, *Lifesongs*; also see https://www.youtube.com/watch?v=KRZaop5ZoJA)
- "As We Now Go" (http://www.seasonsonline.ca/search/results/inventory/Music-Audio/Download-able-Sheet-Music/As-We-Now-Go) or "Alleluia No. 1" (#178, *The Hymnal 1982*)

ARTS CAMP SUNDAY

Planning

Plan your Arts Camp Sunday Worship service with clergy and other parish staff. We recommend that Leaders and Campers present the following portions of the service, which includes incorporating the prepared Offering. Our rector gives us the sermon time for the Arts Camp Offering every year; work with your clergy to decide what is best for your parish.

Here are our recommendations for the service:

Opening Hymn (Campers and Congregation)
* "All Are Welcome"

Hymn of Praise (Campers lead, Congregation learns and joins)
* "Peace Mandala"

Sequence Hymn (Campers Only)
* "Now I Walk in Beauty"

Offertory Anthem (Campers and Congregation)
* "Let There Be Peace on Earth"

Communion Hymn (Campers and Congregation)
* "Prayer of Peace"

Closing Hymn (Campers lead in rounds, Congregation joins)
* "Shalom Chaverim"

Postlude
* "As We Now Go"
* "Alleluia No. 1"

Readings

With clergy approval, we recommend the following readings for the Liturgy of the Word during Arts Camp Sunday Worship:
* Old Testament: Genesis 13:14–18
* Psalm: Psalm 100
* New Testament: Philippians 4:4–8
* Gospel: Luke 6:37–38

Remember to invite confident older Campers to serve as readers for Sunday. Make sure to give them a copy of the reading and have them practice this part of the liturgy during your Friday rehearsal time. Also make sure adult parishioners are not scheduled to read on Arts Camp Sunday.

Eucharistic Prayer 6, from the *Welsh Book of Common Prayer* (http://crucix.com/welsh/communion/cinw-hc-english.pdf, beginning on p. 67), is fitting on Arts Camp Sunday.

PRE-LUNCHTIME STORIES

* Monday: *Small Acts of Kindness* by James Vollbracht
* Tuesday: *Jesus Goes to School* by Carrie Lou Goddard
* Wednesday: *The Legend of the Bluebonnet* by Tomie dePaola or *Giving Thanks: A Native American Good Morning Message* by Chief Jake Swamp
* Thursday: *Moody Cow Meditates* by Kerry Lee MacLean (*Note:* The Mind Jar recipe in the back of this book did *not* work well for us.)
* Friday: *Hindu Creation Story* (This is a colorful, animated, online depiction. Note the correlations to the Christian creation story and to the Holy Trinity. The last few seconds could be slightly frightening for the youngest Campers. You'll find it here: https://www.youtube.com/watch?v=Y9yWwFWpbRo).
* Friday (*alternative*): Stories from *The Little Book of Hindu Deities* by Pixar artist Sanjay Patel

GRACES

The following graces are taken from *The Barefoot Book of Blessings*:
* *Monday:* "Sufi Blessing for Peace," page 12 (Depending on time, you might say this once to Campers, then have them repeat it to you, or go around the circle with each person saying it to the next person.)
* *Tuesday:* "Jewish Mealtime Blessing," page 20 (We changed the word *King* to *Creator* to better fit our parish's emphasis on inclusivity.)

- *Wednesday:* "Native Mealtime Blessing," page 19
- *Thursday:* "Bahai House Blessing," page 23
- *Friday:* "Blessing for Those That You Love," page 8 (We love this because it's fun and wonderfully all-encompassing!)

ART

Our Art Instructor always demonstrates for the Campers and Counselors as he's giving the instructions. This way, most kids know what to do with their materials, and Counselors are prepared to help any Campers who need them. Often, our Counselors will gather three or four Campers who've asked for help at one table and have a group session.

Mandalas

Concept:

A mandala is a circular piece of creative art that is fun to create and promotes a meditative frame of mind. It begins with a circle: the word *mandala* is Sanskrit and translates to "circle."

You might tell the Campers at this time that they'll be creating a mandala through song in Movement sessions throughout the week.

Materials:

- variety of paper and/or cloth for Campers to choose from: card stock, cloth (both preferred), leftover fancy copy paper, butcher paper, tissue paper, etc.
- several compasses, the old-school ones with the point and the pencil holder (*Warn kids that the point is sharp!*)
- pencils (*Golf pencils fit the compass best, but regular pencils are better for the rest of the project.*)
- 12" rulers
- colored pencils and/or thin-point colored markers
- stencils in a variety of shapes/designs (*These are easily found at craft stores.*)
- *Optional:* printed mandala coloring pages for kids who feel intimidated by the idea of creating one from scratch (*The majority of our kids passed right by those in favor of making their own.*)

Directions:

For best results, have all Campers gather around the Art Instructor to watch *and copy* steps 1 and 2. Steps 1 through 4 happen on Monday; Campers then return to their mandalas through the week to color them in and add embellishments.

1. Fold your paper in half lengthwise. Unfold, and fold it in half widthwise. Unfold. Now you have a cross on your paper, and the spot where the two creases meet is the middle.
2. Using the compass, with the point in the middle of the paper, draw a circle. Circles can be large or small, but small circles become very difficult and even tedious to fill in with shape and detail.

For the next steps, have Campers watch, then send them off to work individually.

3. Draw a small shape around the center point; a circle, square, star, diamond, or other polygon works well. Work your way out an inch or two and draw another shape, going around all four of the bisecting lines. It can be the same as the first, but your mandala is more interesting if you change shapes. Keep working your way outward so you end with as many concentric layers as you want.
4. Begin filling each layer with a pattern of lines, geometric shapes, or pictures. Repeat the pattern within the layer, then when you move to the next layer, create a new pattern with a new theme.

Throughout the week, Campers can work on coloring in and adding to their mandalas whenever they've completed another project or are waiting for a turn with their shirt.

A great visual aid for this project can be found at http://www.wikihow.com/Draw-a-Mandala.

Prayer Mats

Concept:

Muslim people are called to prayer five times a day. They try to go to a mosque for prayer, but if there isn't one nearby, they will stop to pray wherever they are. They pray on their knees, bowing down to God, who is called *Allah* in Arabic, by touching their forehead all the way to the ground. They have a prayer mat they lay on the floor or ground whenever they pray.

Materials:

- cloth pre-cut into approximately 18" x 30" rectangles (*Linen, cotton, muslin, and synthetics work well. Felt is not great. Sample books from upholsterers are wonderful, and they are happy to give them away when they're done with them.*)
- fabric shears/scissors, meant for cutting cloth
- cloth strips for weaving
- plastic tapestry needles
- sturdy thread

Directions:

There are two ways for Campers to create their own prayer mats: by weaving them or by cutting and tying the ends to create a fringe. Our Art Instructor happens to own a couple of looms and brought them in so Campers could take turns weaving with them, as well.

Woven Mat

1. Choose your cloth; to weave a mat, you'll need one piece of cloth for your mat plus additional strips.
2. Weaving: starting 1" from either side, cut a line width-wise straight across the cloth, making sure to stop about 1" from the edge. Repeat this step every 1"–2" across your cloth.
3. Pick a cloth strip and thread a tapestry needle, tying the ends of the thread in a knot so you have a double thread with which to sew. Sew the end of the cloth strip to one end of your prayer mat. A couple of stitches are enough to secure the strip, then make sure to knot the thread before cutting it.
4. Weave the strip, in one line on the mat and out the next, until it extends to the other end of the mat. Secure the strip by sewing it as you did the first end, and cut off any excess.

5. Repeat steps 3–4, alternating the lines to make a checkerboard look.

Fringed Mat

1. Choose your cloth; to make a fringed mat, you'll need one piece of cloth.
2. Using fabric scissors, cut about 3" from the edge of the shorter side of the cloth. Cut strips, about 1" each, all the way across this edge, then repeat on the opposite edge. *You will need an even number of strips!*
3. Take two strips that are next to each other and tie them in a solid knot where they meet the prayer mat.
4. Repeat step 3 with all of the strips until you've tied all of them.

Prayer Flags

Note: Purchase inexpensive blank cotton prayer flags for this project. They are available online from http://www.dharmashop.com.

Concept:

Buddhism is the primary faith tradition in Tibet, and prayer flags have been widely used for centuries to promote peace, compassion, goodwill, wisdom, and strength. The idea is that the wind carries the prayers from the flags and spreads them far and wide, bringing benefit to all the world.

There are specific designs and requirements for Tibetan prayer flags, but we had our Campers make their flags fit them and their personal faith journey. Without excessive guidance, what they created was beautiful and unique.

Materials:

- blank prayer flags (*Purchase inexpensive blank cotton prayer flags for this project, available online from* http://www.dharmashop.com. *If you choose not to purchase blank prayer flags, you can make them out of a variety of pieces of cloth and string or cord. Lightweight cloth will look most authentic, and traditionally each flag should be about 6" x 8" and arranged five to a string in a prescribed order: blue, white, red, green, and yellow. A bonus to making your own is that you can wait to tie them after the kids are done decorating them, but in our experience, kids working on strung sets was not a problem.*)
- permanent, fine-tipped markers or fabric paint (*Fabric paint tends to come in very bright colors, while traditional prayer flags are lettered in black, brown, or another dark color.*)
- plastic or newspaper to protect tables
- cord or strong string if making your own strings of flags

Directions:

Note: You might want to print or project pictures of traditional prayer flags for kids to look at before they begin their own.

1. Traditional prayer flags will contain images and text: usually a mantra-style prayer. Invite kids to plan their flag on a piece of paper with a pencil first, before using permanent markers on the cloth itself. Once they're happy with their draft, they can recreate it on their flag.

2. That's it! We found that teaching kids the reason for the flags—they are prayers we send out into the world—and explaining that they should think of a prayer or theme (for example, *peace*) and the image or images they want to include was all they needed. With less direction and more room for creativity, each child's flag was truly unique and individual.

Yarn Prayer Vessels

Concept:

Writing down and keeping one's prayers in a vessel is a powerful way to keep them close in our hearts and minds. It's also a good way for children to relieve stress and worry: once they've written down their worry, handed it to God, and stored it in a prayer vessel, they will noticeably relax and become less distracted by the worry. In Jewish households, a *mezuzah* holds the traditional prayers at the door to the home, and each person who enters acknowledges them by touching their fingers to their mouth and then to the *mezuzah*.

Materials:

- plastic canvas circles from a craft store (*They also come in squares, rectangles, and often you can find crosses.*)
- plastic tapestry needles
- yarn in a wide variety of colors

Directions:

Minimal instructions that illustrate the basics are best for this project and leave room for both learning and creativity.

1. Have each Camper take two of the plastic canvas circles (or other shapes . . . but always two of the *same* shape) and use a marker to mark where they will begin sewing the two shapes together. Have them also mark the spot where they will stop sewing. The idea is to have an opening large enough to slide in a slip of paper containing a prayer, but small enough that the prayer will remain inside until the child chooses to remove it.

2. Demonstrate how to thread the needle with the yarn and how to tie a knot.

3. If they want to, they can sew lines, shapes, and patterns into the middle portions of each circle before they sew the two circles together. Leave the outside row of spaces free; this is where they will sew the two circles together.

4. Demonstrate how to sew a simple stitch that will bind the two circles together along their outside ridge,

starting and stopping at the marked spots to keep an opening in their Prayer Vessel.

Medicine Wheel

Concept:

The Native American medicine wheel symbolizes not only physical well-being, but also overall balance and health in all aspects of life. It is widely used and hung in the homes of Native Americans from many different tribes. The four colors on the wheel bring together the four different directions on a map: white for north, red or yellow for east, yellow or red for south, and black or blue for west. North also represents winter, elders, and wind. East represents children, spring, and fire. South goes with youth, summer, and earth. And West represents parents, fall, and water.

Materials:

- needle-nose pliers
- wire cutters
- sculpting wire, 10 to 16 gauge (The lower number is thicker wire, sturdier, but harder to cut and requiring heavier wire cutters. Adult Volunteers and/or Counselors should pre-cut the sculpting wire into 15" lengths.)
- fine wire, 24 to 28 gauge
- beads in yellow, red, black, white, and one other color of your choice for the center
- yarn, leather, or suede strips
- old, unwanted CDs (They will get scratched!)

Note: Make sure the fine wire gauge you choose will fit into the beads you're using!

Directions:

To see step-by-step instructions with accompanying images, go to http://www.hud.gov/offices/pih/ih/codetalk/planet/connect_medicinewheel.html.

1. Using the needle-nose pliers, bend the sculpting wire into a circle; you can use a CD to guide you. (This step is challenging for younger kids or those with lower fine motor skills; have Adult Volunteers and Counselors ready to help. Put a piece of masking or blue tape around the place where the ends of the wire meet.)
2. Measure the fine wire across the diameter of the circle, with about 2" extra on each side.
3. Wrap the extra 2" around one side of the circle, making sure you wrap around the end to secure the wire. Stretch that wire toward the opposite side of the circle.
4. Pick one color of beads and string them across the wire until you reach about the middle of the circle, leaving space for your two center beads.
5. String the two center beads, then continue stringing the wire with whichever color you choose next.
6. When you reach the opposite side of the circle, wrap the last 2" of wire firmly around the sculpting wire (you can use a piece of tape to hold it temporarily if necessary).
7. Repeat steps 2–6 in a line that goes perpendicular to the first, so your circle is divided into four equal parts. When your second wire meets the first, wrap it once around the first wire to keep them in place.
8. Leaving 2"–3" loose at the top, begin wrapping a piece of yarn tightly around the outside circle. If you've taped wire in place, you can remove the tape when you wrap the yarn around that place. Wrap all the way around, and then tie the ends together at the circle. Cut the remaining yarn, leaving 2"–3" again.
9. Using the extra yarn, tie a loop from which to hang your medicine wheel.

Sand Painting

Concept:

Part of this week's focus on spirituality should be on our connection to the universe; to those who have come before us, those with whom we share this experience, and those who will come when we are a memory. Sand art, done outdoors and temporary by design, is a way to bring this concept to life.

Be aware of pedestrians in the space where you do this project. As an urban parish, we used cones and caution tape to let walkers know there was sand—not to mention children—on the sidewalk outside our building.

It's a good idea to use chalk to delineate a space for each child to work and create to avoid border skirmishes.

Materials:

- cone-shaped coffee filters
- scissors
- craft sand in a variety of colors
- tubs and small paper
- *Optional*: someone with a camera to photograph the art, which will be the only lasting evidence of this project

Directions:

1. Show Campers how to cut a very small piece off the tip of the coffee filters so there will be a small hole for sand to fall through.
2. Campers then fill small cups with several colors of sand to take to their space on the sidewalk, parking lot, or wherever you're doing this project.
3. Campers pour one color at a time into the filter then let it trickle into a picture, design, pattern, or whatever inspires them.
4. Take pictures if you choose, then when Campers have moved on for the day you may have to have a Counselor sweep the sand up if it's in a pedestrian area. If it's safe to leave it, let the elements take care of it.

Zen Gardens

Note: Do this project on the same day you do Sand Paintings, since these are both outdoor projects.

Concept:

Like the Sand Paintings, this is a way to create for the joy of creating, even knowing that what we leave behind will not last. A Zen Garden is a form of meditation as well as creativity widely used by Buddhists around the world.

If you do these projects on the same day, you can divide the group in half and have one group doing Sand Paintings while the other creates Zen Gardens, then switch halfway through the session. This helps in smaller spaces. Campers need to be explicitly told that they will be making their Sand Paintings and Zen Gardens for the joy of making them, and that they will *not* keep them. Assure them that pictures can be taken to help remember what they've created. (For a special needs child who

won't be able to deal with this, you might set aside a special space for that child's work to remain.)

Materials:

- trays, one for each Camper working at the same time (*These could be cardboard box tops such as the lids of shoeboxes, the cardboard pallets that hold a case of drinks, or plastic reusable trays from a thrift or dollar store. You'll want them to hold a layer of sand at least ¼" thick.*)
- sticks and rocks (*If these are not easily found on your parish property, you may want to see about importing them from the yards of your Adult Volunteers. You can purchase rocks from craft stores, but this could become expensive.*)
- plastic forks to use as miniature "rakes"

Directions:

1. Sit down at your tray and breathe deeply in and out, like we do during our meditation time every day. (*If there is any way to bring your meditation music outdoors with you, we highly encourage it for this project.*)
2. Create your Zen Garden however you like with the materials at hand. Rocks can be placed anywhere, and can be spread apart or placed together or even placed atop one another. Use your fork as a rake to make designs in the sand.
3. There is no "finishing" a Zen Garden . . . you can change and adjust it as long as you have time in your

session. If you do feel finished, try meditating on your garden while you breathe in peacefully for the count of three and breathe out peacefully for the count of three.

4. Do try to take pictures of the Campers' gardens both in progress and before they switch to the other group.

Face Painting

Concept:

The Hindu festival called *Holi,* or the Festival of Colors, involves celebrants throwing handfuls of dry paint and spraying colored water at each other, in the air . . . pretty much everywhere! Since we don't wish to go quite that far, face painting in a festival atmosphere on the Friday of camp is a pleasant alternative.

It's important to emphasize to all Campers that they need to work cooperatively. Draw what your partner requests, in the colors s/he chooses.

Materials:

- inexpensive face-painting kits (*Available at craft stores, these come in a wide variety of packages, including sticks that are easy for kids to use. "Party packs" have enough paint for quite a few kids, but you may want to buy extra brushes.*)
- baby wipes and paper towels
- *Optional:* paint shirts or smocks

Directions:

1. We like letting the Campers decorate each other, especially on this last morning of camp when their new friendships have solidified and call for celebration. If you prefer, invite Adult Volunteers and Counselors to paint younger Campers and each other.

2. Play music, preferably international music. *Putumayo* CDs offer a broad selection of music from many cultures (http://www.putumayo.com; also available at iTunes and the Amazon Digital Music Store).

3. If you have projection capabilities, show pictures of *Holi* celebrations.

Tie-Dye

Note: We do this for every year's camp!

Concept:

Our shirts bring us together as a community. Each starts the same, then proclaims how each of us is our own special and unique child of God. No two will ever look alike once they've been dyed! We thank God for camp, for color, for the magic that happens when we combine colors and when we appear to make a mess. We present these shirts to each other, to the congregation, and to God on Sunday when we make our Offering at worship. And we keep the shirts, some of us year after year, to remember the joy, faith, fun, and fellowship of each year's camp.

Materials:

- T-shirts; preordered from a printer (see Chapter 2: *2–4 Weeks before Camp,* p. 18)
- rubber bands for tying shirts
- dye kit including squirt bottles (*Cleaner and safer than vat dyeing!*)
- gallon plastic zipper bags
- paint shirts or trash bag ponchos to cover kids (*optional*)
- non-latex gloves
- tarps
- crates: With 24–28 enrollment, we use two crates.
- large tubs, big enough to hold two overturned crates with a bit of room between

Notes:

- We use and highly recommend dyes, fixers, and instructions from Grateful Dyes Inc. They have everything you need plus great instructions, and they ship worldwide. Here is their website: http://www.grateful-dyes.com.
- You can also find tie-dye kits at most hobby stores. Make sure you buy a kit that comes with specific instructions and includes the fixers you need to mix the dyes. You'll want to have everything ready to go when the kids dye their shirts, including three squirt bottles per station with red, yellow, and blue dye. Some kits have you soak shirts in a solution prior to

dying; you'll want your Art Instructor(s) and Counselors to make sure this is done ahead of time.

- Instructions and diagrams for dyeing shirts in specific patterns are available from Grateful Dyes as well as all over the Internet!

Directions:

Note: We do this outside on the lawn and still spread tarps . . . this is a messy activity! Putting the tied shirts on an overturned milk crate that in turn is standing in a large metal tray or plastic tub helps catch excess dye. Before you begin, have Senior Counselors mark each shirt with the Campers' initials; you should have compiled a list when you ordered, using the Campers' registration packets to determine each child's size.

1. On Monday, once other art projects are well under way, take small groups and hand out their shirts. Show kids how to twist their shirts and then secure them with rubber bands, helping them as needed.
2. Store the tied shirts in a large tub.
3. On Tuesday and/or Wednesday, have a tie-dye station set up outdoors, close to a door that leads to the Art space, if possible. You want at least one adult and a Counselor for every four Campers who are tie-dying.
4. Have Campers put on gloves and paint shirts/ponchos, if desired.
5. Give Campers their tied shirts and have them place them on of the overturned milk crates in the tub.
6. Using one color at a time, use the squirt bottles to saturate the part of the shirt where you want that color. If you want a very colorful shirt, you need to really soak the area.
7. Repeat step 6 using different colors on the rest of the shirt.
8. Turn the shirt over and repeat steps 6 and 7 on this side. (If children want their shirts to be similar on both sides, have them turn them over as they do each color and section.)
9. Place the finished shirt in a gallon zipper bag and seal it.
10. The Art Instructors will need to rinse the shirts and then run them through a washing machine before

they're finished. For a large camp we suggest that the adults all take a batch of shirts home and help out!

11. *Hold onto the shirts until Sunday!* We always show the kids their finished shirts on Friday, but then collect them again to hand out on Sunday morning.

MUSIC

This is a camp for which having a strong musical-instruction team is very helpful.

We use several chants and rounds, which the Campers then present and teach to the congregation on Arts Camp Sunday. Our Choir Director and Arts Camp Music Instructor just happens to play Native American flute and drums, and brought those talents along with many others to camp. When choosing a team for this camp, we strongly recommend that you find a Music Instructor with an interest in and talent for international music so your music sessions will be as rich as possible. Another avenue would be to spread the word that you're looking for volunteers who might have special knowledge of or talent for any one of the musical traditions you'll explore, and ask if they can stop by Arts Camp on the day you're exploring that tradition.

You might also check out this website: http://www. sacredmusicradio.org.

Remember that each day's session should include musical Games and Movement/Drama, as well as instruction.

We correlate our Music as much as possible with the faith we are exploring each day, as follows:

- *Monday:*
  Play a recording of the Muslim call to prayer, then compare and contrast it to Christian chants such as Gregorian Monks and Songs of Taizé. Clearly, you'll want some technology to do this. We found a wide variety of calls to prayer online, as well as for purchase from iTunes and the Amazon Digital Music Store. Likewise with Taizé and Gregorian chant. So an MP3 player and docking station, a CD player, or even a projection system will be useful. With projection,

you can even show video of the call to prayer and monks chanting.

Teach Campers about chant as a musical device, and how it's created. Think of some of the sung settings for The Lord's Prayer, and how psalms can be chanted as well. Then have them try a game in which they introduce themselves through a simple chant of three or four notes, chanting their name, age, and one important thing they wanted to tell about themselves. The Music Instructor should go first to model how to do this. While all Campers are to be encouraged, no child should be forced to take a turn. We always like to come back to that child later in case s/he feels more prepared after listening to others.

Plan to teach Campers the first two verses of *Prayer of Peace* on Monday, as well.

- *Tuesday:*
As we were exploring Judaism, Campers began to learn the round "Shalom Chaverim." You can find many examples of this traditional song online. You can find sheet music here: http://www.mtrs.co.uk/rounds.htm. Here is a straightforward and easy way to hear the song and its timing on YouTube: https://www.youtube.com/watch?v=KRZaop5ZoJA. Once Campers know the lyrics and melody, you can start having them practice singing in rounds.

- *Wednesday:*
As we explored Native American drums and dance, we began learning the chant "Now I Walk in Beauty," which connects wonderfully to "Prayer for Peace." Interfaith Peace Camp explores the ways our faith traditions bring us together rather than divide us, and connections like these emphasize those relationships. Learn and practice both "Prayer for Peace" and "Now I Walk in Beauty" as part of Wednesday's Music session.

For Native Americans, tribal use of percussion and vocal song plays a vital role in ceremony and storytelling. As with liturgy in Christian worship, ceremony and storytelling are human rituals for remembering and teaching the stories common to our ancestors for generation upon generation. For American Indians, dance is also a vital component of ceremony and prayer.

If you don't happen to have a musician who plays Native American flute and drums, this is another opportunity to look in your community for someone with those talents. If all else fails, the Internet is a solid backup. You can find hundreds of videos and examples of Native American drums and dance online. There are also recordings of Native American flute and drums widely available. Once Campers have seen and heard some examples, have them try their own drum circle. Hands on the floor or on knees, actual drums if you have them, or rhythm sticks (on carpet!) are all fun ways to try this. Starting with the adult, one person in the circle begins to beat a specific and repeated rhythm, which the rest of the circle then practices. Once the whole circle is drumming together, move to the next person and have him or her change the beat, which everyone then must follow. Continue until you've gone around the circle.

A variation would be to have a few kids drum while others make up their own storytelling dance to the beat of the drums. Try with a well-known fairy tale like "The Boy Who Cried Wolf," or a bible story like Noah's Ark. Give kids parts from the stories and have them dance the story while you (or a Camper) narrate it.

- *Thursday:*
Play Buddhist chants for the Campers, and connect this chanting to what they heard earlier in the week. You might also try to borrow a bell, inverted cymbals, and drums from a local temple, if you have one, for children to see and hear. If you're using the schedule for a small or medium-sized Arts Camp, this is your last Music session for the week, so this is also the time to play Hindu music for the kids, and to lead a discussion as to the similarities and differences in all the types of music they've heard this week.

Also on Thursday practice both "Prayer of Peace" and "Now I Walk in Beauty," and sing through "Let

There Be Peace on Earth" at least once. If, on Sunday, you're inviting the congregation to sing this with you, then you only need the Campers to have heard and sung it once for familiarity. This is our recommendation, as you undoubtedly have parishioners who remember that song fondly and will enjoy singing it again. There is a heartwarming story about the beginnings of this song's widespread popularity at http://www.jan-leemusic.com/Site/History.html.

MOVEMENT/DRAMA

The resource book *I Open My Eyes to You: Dances of Universal Peace* from the Children's Global Peace Project is critical for the movement sessions of this camp as they are outlined here. For $30 (including shipping) you get a book of dances, activities, and games, plus a CD. Our Movement Instructor chose dances from the book according to her own talents and preferences, and the kids loved them. We also used some of the games for the end of our Arts Camp days.

On pages 44–45 of this book is a Peace Greeting. Use this activity, with the day's peace greeting, every day. Monday you'll begin with *"Peace be with you, and with you be peace,"* and once the Campers have that you'll add *"Asalaam Alaikum, Walaikum Asalaam."* Tuesday you'll teach the Hebrew addition, then break the Campers into three groups doing all three parts. Have the Instructor start each group, one after another, moving on only when the previous group has their part going well. Having an Adult Volunteer or Counselor in each group helps. Doing this in the circle dance described in the book is a nice way to begin each day's movement session.

Along with beginning our sessions with this Peace Greeting, our Movement/Drama Instructor also helped kids build a musical Peace Mandala, which we then used as our Hymn of Praise in the Sunday service. This sounds more difficult than it is. The Campers are learning about and hearing examples of chants all week; they are more able than you might think to create their own chants. Start on Monday by creating a chant with

the words *Dona Nobis Pacem* (Latin for "give us peace"). Encourage Campers to keep this chant simple; two to three notes is all you need. Tuesday, make sure everyone remembers and can sing the first part, then add a new, complementary chant for the words *Shalom, Salaam*. Once everyone can sing each chant, combine them by having half the group sing one and the other half sing the other. Each day this week, practice the chants you've created, then create and learn a new chant or the following peace words: *Om Mani Padme Hum, May the Great Spirit Walk with You*, and *Shanti, Shanti*. You'll want to add *Om Mani Padme Hum* on Thursday, as Friday is your rehearsal day. Make sure the children understand that each of these words or phrases means peace or that peace is possible. This is why we call it a Peace Mandala.

Note: If you've divided your Campers into two or more groups for Movement/Drama sessions, as we recommend, you'll need to be mindful of having each group's input for the chants in your Peace Mandala. You might take turns, so each group has at least one chant included in the final product. Or your Movement/Drama Instructor and Accompanist might, at the end of each day, work together to tweak the chants that were offered that day into one chant that fits with the others and is easy to learn. Remember that for this exercise to work, you want each chant to contain only a very few notes that work together to create a rich sound.

If creating a Peace Mandala feels too daunting, you could certainly teach and use another of the many offerings from *I Open My Eyes to You*.

In addition to these two musical activities, your Movement sessions should include other dances and games you've picked from the resource *I Open My Eyes to You: Dances of Universal Peace*. If you choose not to purchase this resource, Dances of Universal Peace has a YouTube channel where they've posted 30 videos of different dances, but you will miss the sheet music, games, and so much more included in the book.

For Sunday's Offering, on Thursday an Adult Volunteer sits down with each group and invites each Camper to share at least one important realization, learning, or discovery s/he has from Arts Camp. Explain that what they say now should be something they feel strongly about teaching the congregation on Sunday. Scribe their thoughts as they give them to you. After Camp Thursday, before Camp Friday, you'll need to put all of these lines together in a script with each child's name and the line(s) they've offered. Pick and choose so there is a flow, as this will be a collective homily offered by the Campers to the congregation.

For Friday, you need a copy of this homily for each Camper, with his or her line(s) highlighted. At Friday's rehearsal, line Campers up in front of the altar (or wherever they will stand to speak), in order of speakers in the script. When they give this Offering to the congregation, they will simply pass a handheld microphone from one child to the next as they speak. *Note:* Once the Campers are lined up and rehearsing speaking their parts, have Counselors write their names on blue painter's tape and mark their spots on the floor for Sunday.

POPSICLES/SNACK, GAMES, AND CLOSING THE CAMP DAY

See Chapter 6 (p. 35) for the specifics of how to end the day and Appendix 3 (p. 117) for a list of tried-and-true camp games.

FRIDAY AFTERNOON

Before you pray and sing, which should be the last act of the last day of Arts Camp, you may want to leave time for an evaluation. A simple evaluation form can be found in Appendix 2 (p. 114).

You'll also want to make sure Campers take home the things they brought with them at the beginning of the week and that have accumulated throughout camp: water bottles, beach towels, sweaters and sweatshirts, hats and sunglasses. Also send home any art projects that you do *not* want to use or display on Sunday. Keep tie-dye shirts and everything else they will wear or display on Sunday.

You'll want your Art Instructor(s) and Counselors to spend time following the last Art session on Friday setting up a display of the Campers' creations so that is in place for Sunday.

Finally, send a note home with each family on Friday afternoon thanking them for bringing their children to camp and giving them details on the Sunday service, including what time Campers should arrive. You want time for Campers to put on their tie-dye shirts and to come to the choir loft to practice before the service begins. A sample of this note home can be found with the forms in Appendix 2 (p. 113). We copy this note on brightly colored paper and place it next to the sign-out sheet for parents to see and take when they come to pick up their Campers.

As with every day of Arts Camp, but especially on Friday, you'll want your Counselors to stay later so they can help you put camp away!

Throughout the week, we have parents who tend to arrive to pick up their children a little early, so they've seen and heard our closing prayer and song. On Friday, once we've given instructions for taking things home and final cleanup, invite parents and caregivers to join the circle at this time. Then try not to get emotional as you sing your goodbye blessing and realize that Arts Camp is over for the year.

CHAPTER 11

Arts Camp: Saints and Holy Helpers

 IN THE WAKE OF THE DEVASTATING TRAGEDY at Sandy Hook Elementary School in December 2012, we all saw the following quote, which is attributed to Fred Rogers:

> When I was a boy and I would see scary things in the news, my mother would say to me, "Look for the helpers. You will always find people who are helping."

This camp explores the people throughout history who are remembered and even revered for being the helpers. We also strive to help children connect to those people personally as they begin to view themselves as a vital part of the communion of saints.

We started on the Monday of camp with our own parish's patron saint, Barnabas. If your parish is named for a saint, that's a logical place from which to jump into the pool of Saints and Holy Helpers. If not, there are an abundance of wonderful saints from which to choose!

The hymn "I Sing a Song of the Saints of God" is another lens of focus for this camp; we spend Tuesday and Wednesday mornings learning about the *doctor*, the *queen*, and the rest, right up to Ignatius of Antioch who was *slain by a fierce wild beast*.

MORNING PROGRAM

Remember to have the sign-in/sign-out sheet ready for parents and caregivers, and nametags and markers for all Campers for the morning check-in time.

Also have scripture passages and quotes printed on card stock and either hanging up or ready to be hung up once you've used them in your morning sessions.

Always call camp together in the mornings with a song. "This is the Day" is wonderful for gathering Campers in the morning, and "Hallelujah! Praise ye the Lord!" works beautifully for transitions, including ending the Morning Program and heading off to Art, Music, and Drama sessions (see Chapter 3, p. 23).

Introduce yourself and do an introduction activity (we offer one, Who Are We? found in Appendix 3, p. 121), then say a prayer for your day together:

> May we be filled with loving-kindness.
> May we be well.
> May we be peaceful and at ease.
> May we be happy.

I purchased the following books for this camp, in addition to those listed below under "Pre-Lunchtime Stories":

- *I Sing a Song of the Saints of God* by Lesbia Scott, illustrated by Judith Gwyn Brown
- *Peter Claver, Patron Saint of Slaves* by Julia Durango and Rebecca Garcia-Franco (this book is printed in English and Spanish)
- *The Monk Who Grew Prayer* by Claire Brandenburg

We were also able to borrow several books about Saint Francis and other saints from our clergy.

Before camp begins, have the following quotes prepared on card stock, as well as the Mr. Rogers quote at the beginning of this chapter:

- If you want to make peace with your enemy, you have to work with your enemy. Then she becomes your partner. (Nelson Mandela)
- For every minute you remain angry, you give up sixty seconds of peace of mind. (Ralph Waldo Emerson)
- We can never obtain peace with the outer world until we make peace with ourselves. (The Dalai Lama)

- We are what we believe we are. (C. S. Lewis)
- If God can work through me, God can work through anyone. (St. Francis of Assisi)
- Where there is charity and wisdom, there is neither fear nor ignorance. (St. Francis of Assisi)
- Since love grows within you, so beauty grows. For love is the beauty of the soul. (St. Augustine)
- God loves each of us as if there were only one of us. (St. Augustine)
- May God protect me from gloomy saints. (St. Theresa of Avila)
- The feeling remains that God is on the journey, too. (St. Theresa of Avila)
- Christ beside me, Christ before me, Christ behind me, Christ within me, Christ beneath me, Christ above me. (St. Patrick)
- What good is speed if the brain has oozed out on the way? (St. Jerome)
- Teach us to give and not to count the cost. (St. Ignatius)
- Be generous to the orphans and those in need. Those to whom our Lord has been liberal ought not to be stingy. We shall one day find in Heaven as much rest and joy as we ourselves have dispensed in this life. (St. Ignatius)

- *Monday:*
  After you've sung and played an introductory game, ask Campers what they know about Saints. Again, if you're sitting in a building called St. Somebody's, that may be one of the first comments you'll hear. This is the time to tell Campers the stories of that saint. Check *Lesser Feasts and Fasts* and the Revised Common Lectionary site (http://www.lectionary-page.net) for information and prayers about most Saints.

  St. Nicholas is likely to appear in this first discussion, and children never tire of hearing about the saint who inspired—or became, depending on your interpretation of the legend—Santa Claus. We took the path of telling Campers in detail about the legends surrounding the historical figure, St. Nicholas, the Bishop of Myra. This story is widely available in books and on websites, and details can vary, but the common thread is that St. Nicholas was a third-century bishop in what is now Turkey. Born to a wealthy family, Nicholas spent his inheritance following Christ's call to sell what we own and give to the needy. He preferred to give anonymously, at least according to the stories, and found ways to sneak gifts into people's homes. There is a rather gruesome story of Nicholas saving three boys after they'd been murdered and hidden in a butcher's barrel or pickling tub; we leave it to you whether and how to share that one with children! For more—and as accurate as possible—information, as well as game and activity suggestions about St. Nicholas, go to the St. Nicholas Center's website: http://www.stnicholascenter.org.

  St. Francis is the other figure you need to teach the children about today, as you'll use his prayer throughout the week. Information about St. Francis abounds, and you'll give Campers a story about St. Francis before lunch on Monday.

- *Tuesday:*
  Begin to teach the children about the saints mentioned in the hymn "I Sing a Song of the Saints of God." The hymn was written by Lesbia Scott as part of a collection of hymns she composed for her own children. The specific saints mentioned in the hymn are as follows:
  — *And one was a doctor* = Luke the Apostle and Physician
  — *And one was a queen* = Queen Margaret of Scotland
  — *And one was a shepherdess on the green* = Joan of Arc
  — *And one was a soldier* = Martin of Tours
  — *And one was a priest* = John Donne
  — *And one was slain by a fierce wild beast* = Ignatius of Antioch
  Tuesday you will also tell the children the stories of Sts. Luke, Margaret, and Joan.

- *Wednesday:*
  Move on to Sts. Martin, John, and Ignatius. Note that John Donne does not lend himself brilliantly to young

people. He was a ponderous writer and thinker, and we told the Campers simply that he wrote to teach people about God and about heavenly life after death.

- *Thursday:*
For Thursday, we came up with a list of saints who protect us, with a range from the very comforting to the rather silly, which the kids of course loved!

St. Christopher is the patron saint of travelers and gardeners, who also protects us from lightning.

St. Christina the Astonishing is the patron of those with mental illness.

St. Jude is the patron saint of lost causes and those who feel hopeless.

St. Kentigern protects us from bullies and mean words: the Campers loved the idea of standing up to a child who is being unkind by saying, "You can't hurt me because I have St. Kentigern on my side!" Whether any of them actually went on to attempt it, we have not heard.

St. Albinus is the patron saint of pirates, while St. Anthony is believed to help us find missing people as well as lost objects.

There are patron saints for just about every job you can think of, and even a designated saint who protects pig farmers: St. Malo.

There will certainly be children in your camp who carry saints' names, and it's fun to explore those. Be careful, though, not to dwell too deeply as those who are not named after saints could feel left out.

Hymns and Songs

- "This is the Day" (#219, *Lift Every Voice and Sing II*)
- "Hallelujah! Praise ye the Lord!" (#179, *Lifesongs*)
- "I Sing a Song of the Saints of God" (#293, *The Hymnal 1982*)
- "Prayer of Peace" (http://www.hymnary.org/text/peace_before_us_peace_behind_us)
- "Arky Arky" (http://www.hymnary.org/hymn/SWM/66)
- "I'm Gonna Sing" (# 117, *Lift Every Voice and Sing II*)

- "Oh When the Saints Go Marchin' In" (http://www.hymnary.org)
- "Channel of Your Peace" (http://www.hymnary.org)
- "The Servant Song" (#94, *My Heart Sings Out*; #539, *The New Century Hymnal*)
- "The Twelve Saints of Arts Camp" (Original, to the tune of "The Twelve Days of Christmas")
- "As We Now Go" (available from Seasons online at http://www.seasonsonline.ca/search/results/inventory/Music-Audio/Downloadable-Sheet-Music/As-We-Now-Go) or "Alleluia No. 1" (#178, *The Hymnal 1982*)

ARTS CAMP SUNDAY

Planning

Plan your Arts Camp Sunday Worship service with clergy and other parish staff. We recommend that Leaders and Campers present the following portions of the service, which includes incorporating the prepared Offering. Our rector gives us the sermon time for the Arts Camp offering every year; work with your clergy to decide what is best for your parish.

Here are our recommendations for the service:

Opening Hymn: (Campers and Congregation)
- "I Sing a Song of the Saints of God"

Hymn of Praise: (Campers and Congregation)
- "Hallelujah! Praise ye the Lord!"

Sequence Hymn: (Campers and Congregation)
- "Prayer for Peace"

Offertory Anthem: (Campers and Congregation)
- "O When the Saints Go Marching In"

Communion Hymn: (Campers Only)
- "Make Me a Channel of Your Peace"

Closing Hymn: (Campers and Congregation)
- "The Servant Song"

Postlude:
- "As We Now Go"
- "Alleluia No. 1"

Readings

With clergy approval, we recommend the following readings for the Liturgy of the Word during Arts Camp Sunday Worship:

- Old Testament: Isaiah 6:1–8
- Psalm: Psalm 100
- New Testament: Philippians 4:4–8
- Gospel: Matthew 5:3–10

Remember to invite confident older Campers to serve as readers for Sunday. Make sure to give them a copy of the reading and have them practice this part of the liturgy during your Friday rehearsal time. Also make sure adult parishioners are not scheduled to read on Arts Camp Sunday.

Eucharistic Prayer 6, from the Welsh Book of Common Prayer (http://crucix.com/welsh/communion/cinw-hc-english.pdf, beginning on page 67), is fitting on Arts Camp Sunday.

PRE-LUNCHTIME STORIES:

- Monday: *Saint Francis,* created by Kathleen Crevasse in a beautiful Godly Play style story (found in Appendix 1, p. 97)
- *Note:* You will need to prepare ahead and create the St. Francis box with the items listed in the story. Then you'll have it for St. Francis day at your parish, too!
- Tuesday: *Clown of God* by Tomie dePaola
- Wednesday: *A Saint and His Lion* by Elaine Murray Stone and Cecile Sharrott
- Thursday: *Brigid's Cloak* by Bryce Milligan and Helen Cann
- Friday: *St. George and the Dragon* by Margaret Hodges and Trina Schart Hyman

GRACES

From the prayer cube mentioned in Chapter 5 (p. 33), we found these graces fitting:

God, bless this food
We are about to receive.
Give bread to those who hunger,
And hunger for charity and justice
To us who have bread.
Amen.

Bless our food,
Dear God we pray,
And bless us, too
throughout this day.
Keep us safe and close to You,
Keep us just in all we do.
Amen.

ART

Stained Glass Windows

Concept:

Symbols and shields have always been used to commemorate the saints. Each of the twelve apostles has a personalized shield, and most of the saints have at least one if not many symbols attributed to them. This is a project that allows children to come up with one or more symbols they would choose for themselves.

If your building has traditional stained glass windows, most likely there are saints' shields incorporated into those windows. Take Campers for a tour of these windows and talk about what you see there.

If stained glass is not a part of your building, there are plenty of pictures to be found online or in reference books from the library.

Another source for ideas would be the illuminated manuscripts that monks created in the middle ages. Again, an Internet search of "illuminated manuscripts" or a reference book from the Art History section of a library should provide examples.

Materials:

- shrinkable plastic sheets *(available at craft stores)* or recycled clear plastic containers *(You need at least 8"* x 12" flat sheets.)

- masking tape
- permanent markers, both fine- and wide-tipped
- hole punches
- ribbon

Directions for Campers:

1. What animals, flowers, designs, or other symbols would be important in a stained glass window dedicated *to you?* Design your own stained glass window, starting by creating a sketch on paper with pencil so you can make changes and adjustments until it's just the way you want it.

2. Once your drawing is exactly what you want, place a sheet of plastic over it. You might want to secure the paper to the plastic with masking tape so it won't wiggle once you start tracing.

3. Using permanent markers, trace your pencil drawing onto your plastic sheet. Take time to use lots of color and detail.

4. Once you are sure you've added as much as you want to your "window," use the hole punch to make holes in the upper left and right corners.

5. Now ask an Adult Volunteer or a Counselor to place your finished shield on a tray and place it in the toaster oven at 325°. Watch your shield constantly, because it won't take long to shrink. The plastic will shrink and thicken, hardening in the process, while your picture perfectly miniaturizes itself. (If the sides begin to roll up, ask the Adult Volunteer or Counselor to simply use a spatula to push it flat again.)

6. Once your shield has shrunk, an Adult Volunteer or a Counselor will take it out of the oven and set it aside to cool.

7. When your shield has cooled, pick a ribbon color and tie the ribbon through the holes you punched in the top, so you can hang your stained glass in a window.

Saints-in-Action Dioramas

Concept:

As Campers learn about more and more saints and their stories, they create an action scene to illustrate favorites. Campers enjoy working in pairs or trios for this project, which can extend several days as they add more stories from each day's exploration.

Materials:

- Sculpey® modeling clay in a variety of colors (*Sculpey® is a modeling clay that retains its pliability until it's baked. So Campers can adjust and arrange their model saints and animals and scenery as much as needed.*)
- shoeboxes and other small to midsize boxes for backgrounds
- markers
- various tools for sculpting clay such as plastic knives and forks, toothpicks, chopsticks, etc.
- cookie trays
- aluminum foil

Directions:

Note: This is a project where less is more in terms of instructions. You might like to make an example ahead of time: for example, make a St. Francis statuette with a small wolf by his side or a few birds on his arms. Kids are intrinsically creative, and when we over-instruct them we can shut down that creativity.

1. To start, ask, "What is a diorama?" You will likely have fourth through sixth graders who have made them for school and can explain. In the unlikely chance there is not, define a diorama as a model, in this case miniaturized, of a scene. Point out that natural history museums have dioramas of animals standing in their natural habitats. A diorama uses a combination of models and a backdrop, which provides scenery.

2. Explain that this week you will be making dioramas to represent scenes from your favorite stories about the saints.

3. Have cookie trays covered in aluminum foil set aside. Campers set their finished pieces on these trays. Our kids were remarkably good at remembering which of the several St. Georges and Dragons were theirs, but it's a good idea to have them carve initials in the bottoms of their pieces to help keep track.

4. Cook the pieces according to the package instructions. We did ours every day to keep up with Campers'

demands, and every day the kids were thrilled to see their finished creations and make new ones to add.

Saints-Medallion Necklaces

Concept:

Small silver or gold pendants have long been popular gifts among Catholics and Anglicans. Many of us still wear a St. Christopher medallion when we travel, and others wear a saint's pendant as a symbol of protection. Between us, the adult leadership of our camp found we owned a variety of St. Christopher and Blessed Virgin pendants, along with one depicting St. Barnabas and another of St. Vincent. We brought these to the Art session and passed them among Campers, then told them they'd be making their own versions from modeling clay. If you aren't familiar with these medallions, a simple Internet search yields an abundance of pictures.

Materials:

- Sculpey® in a variety of colors
- toothpicks
- ribbon
- cookie trays
- aluminum foil

Directions:

Having your own example already made to show Campers helps them picture what they'll be creating. Once they have seen examples of pendants depicting saints, offer these instructions:

1. Choose a saint. It could be a saint you're named for, or one you've liked learning about this week.

2. Using the clay, build a round base for your medallion. A circle or oval are both fine. Use a toothpick to make a hole big enough to string a ribbon through at the top—not too close to the edge, so it won't tear or break.

3. From there, carve into the clay your favorite saint and/or any symbol you feel fits that saint.

4. When you're finished, use a toothpick to carve your initials on the back of your pendant and place it on the cookie tray for baking.

5. The Art Instructor or a Counselor will bake your pendant for you.

Bake according to the instructions on the packaging, and return them to the Campers the following day. Save these medallions at church for kids to wear for Arts Camp Sunday Worship.

Tie-Dye:

Concept:

Our shirts bring us together as a community. Each starts the same, then proclaims how each of us is our own special and unique child of God. No two will ever look alike once they've been dyed! We thank God for camp, for color, for the magic that happens when we combine colors and when we appear to make a mess. We present these shirts to each other, to the congregation, and to God on Sunday when we make our Offering at worship. And we keep the shirts, some of us year after year, to remember the joy, faith, fun, and fellowship of each year's camp.

Materials:

- T-shirts; preordered from a printer (see Chapter 2: *2–4 Weeks before Camp*, p. 18)
- rubber bands for tying shirts
- dye kit including squirt bottles (*Cleaner and safer than vat dyeing!*)
- gallon plastic zipper bags
- paint shirts or trash bag ponchos to cover kids (*optional*)

- non-latex gloves
- tarps
- crates: With 24–28 enrollment, we use two crates.
- large tubs, big enough to hold two overturned crates with a bit of room between

Notes:

- We use and highly recommend dyes, fixers, and instructions from Grateful Dyes Inc. They have everything you need plus great instructions, and they ship worldwide. Here is their website: http://www.grateful-dyes.com.
- You can also find tie-dye kits at most hobby stores. Make sure you buy a kit that comes with specific instructions and includes the fixers you need to mix the dyes. You'll want to have everything ready to go when the kids dye their shirts, including three squirt bottles per station with red, yellow, and blue dye. Some kits have you soak shirts in a solution prior to dying; you'll want your Art Instructor(s) and Counselors to make sure this is done ahead of time.
- Instructions and diagrams for dyeing shirts in specific patterns are available from Grateful Dyes as well as all over the Internet!

Directions:

Note: We do this outside on the lawn and still spread tarps . . . this is a messy activity! Putting the tied shirts on an overturned milk crate that in turn is standing in a large metal tray or plastic tub helps catch excess dye. Before you begin, have Senior Counselors mark each shirt with the Campers' initials; you should have compiled a list when you ordered, using the Campers' registration packets to determine each child's size.

1. On Monday, once other art projects are well under way, take small groups and hand out their shirts. Show kids how to twist their shirts and then secure them with rubber bands, helping them as needed.
2. Store the tied shirts in a large tub.
3. On Tuesday and/or Wednesday, have a tie-dye station set up outdoors, close to a door that leads to the Art space, if possible. You want at least one adult and a Counselor for every four Campers who are tie-dying.
4. Have Campers put on gloves and paint shirts/ponchos, if desired.
5. Give Campers their tied shirts and have them place them on one of the overturned milk crates in the tub.
6. Using one color at a time, use the squirt bottles to saturate the part of the shirt where you want that color. If you want a very colorful shirt, you need to really soak the area.
7. Repeat step 6 using different colors on the rest of the shirt.
8. Turn the shirt over and repeat steps 6 and 7 on this side. (If children want their shirts to be similar on both sides, have them turn them over as they do each color and section.)
9. Place the finished shirt in a gallon zipper bag and seal it.
10. The Art Instructors will need to rinse the shirts and then run them through a washing machine before they're finished. For a large camp we suggest that the adults all take a batch of shirts home and help out!
11. *Hold onto the shirts until Sunday!* We always show the kids their finished shirts on Friday, but then collect them again to hand out on Sunday morning.

You may note that there are fewer projects this week than other Arts Camp weeks. This is simply because the dioramas and shrink art were so popular that Campers easily filled their days with them. If you need supplemental material, there are many projects in the other camps that are popular enough to bring back again and again: God's Eyes and Friendship Beads to trade on Friday are some of our kids' favorites.

Also, our Art Instructor had two inexpensive, small peg looms and brought them for anyone who was interested in trying weaving. This wasn't an official "Saints" project, but did tie in with the historic feel that came with exploring so many people who lived so long ago and the tapestries and textiles that were so vital to their lives.

MUSIC

In this week's Arts Camp, the main focus in Music sessions will be on creating original lyrics for a song about

12 saints of your choosing. The lyrics for our version are provided below, and you have the option of teaching the stories of these saints and using that version. But we hope you'll consider changing at least a few lines by encouraging your Campers to make this song their own. You'll have to change the second verse unless your church is actually called St. Barnabas. The tune is to "The Twelve Days of Christmas."

Our kids decided that Jesus is the Saint of Saints, and insisted he finish the song as the Twelfth Saint of Arts Camp. Who were we to argue with that logic?

On Monday, teach Campers the first three verses, so they'll begin to understand the idea of adapting a favorite Christmas song to fit this week's theme. Once they've sung this first bit through a couple of times, ask them about the saints we talked about this morning. What did they learn, what parts of the stories stand out to them? Help them fit their words into the rhythm of the song to write a new verse or two.

Tuesday, teach them about Saint Kateri Tekakwitha ("*Cat*-er-eye Ti-*kaw*-kwith-ah"), who is one of few North Americans and the first Native American to be sainted. Kateri Tekakwitha was born to the Mohawk tribe in New York State in 1656. Her mother died of smallpox, which Kateri also caught when she was very small. She was baptized as a young woman and spent her life in prayer, devotion, and the care of the sick in the colony of Christian Indians where she lived. She was sainted in 1980. While the conversion of American Indians by seventeenth-century missionaries is a complex and often violent story, dwelling on Kateri's devotion and her status as the first Native American to be sainted can keep controversy out of your explorations.

"THE TWELVE SAINTS OF ARTS CAMP"

written by David Bell and the children of St. Barnabas Arts Camp, June 2014

Let us sing to the saints a song of glory,
To Mary, the mother of God.

And to Barnabas the preacher,
For whom we are named;

Saint Barnabas and Mary, the mother of God.

And to Saint George the mighty
Who fought a dragon;

Saint George, Saint Barnabas, and Mary, the mother of God.

And to Saint Cecilia,
The saint of music;

Saint Cecilia, Saint George, Saint Barnabas, and Mary, the mother of God.

And to our most beloved saint of animals,
Saint Francis! (*This is the "Five golden rings" part.*)

Saint Cecilia, Saint George, Saint Barnabas, and Mary, the mother of God.

And to Kateri Tekakwitha,
A Native American;

Saint Kateri, Saint Francis!

Saint Cecilia, Saint George, Saint Barnabas, and Mary, the mother of God.

And to Patrick the blessed,
Who was caught by pirates;

Saint Patrick, Saint Kateri, Saint Francis!

Saint Cecilia, Saint George, Saint Barnabas, and Mary, the mother of God.

And to Margaret the queen,
Who fed the poor;

Saint Margaret, Saint Patrick, Saint Kateri, Saint Francis!

Saint Cecilia, Saint George, Saint Barnabas, and Mary, the mother of God.

And to Tekla from Africa,
Who healed a lion;

Saint Tekla, Saint Margaret, Saint Patrick, Saint Kateri, Saint Francis!

Saint Cecilia, Saint George, Saint Barnabas, and Mary, the mother of God.

And to Joan of Arc,
Who fought for righteousness;

Saint Joan, Saint Tekla, Saint Margaret, Saint Patrick, Saint Kateri, Saint Francis!

Saint Cecilia, Saint George, Saint Barnabas, and Mary, the mother of God.

And to Brigid the healer,
Whose cloak shone with stars;

Saint Brigid, Saint Joan, Saint Tekla, Saint Margaret, Saint Patrick, Saint Kateri, Saint Francis!

Saint Cecilia, Saint George, Saint Barnabas, and Mary, the mother of God.

And to Jesus our Savior,
The Son of God;

Jesus Christ, Saint Brigid, Saint Joan, Saint Tekla, Saint Margaret, Saint Patrick, Saint Kateri, Saint Francis!

Saint Cecilia, Saint George, Saint Barnabas, and Mary, the mother of God.

You'll also teach Campers two other songs this week: "O When the Saints Go Marchin' In" and "Make Me a Channel of Your Peace." If you have access to shakers, tambourines, cymbals, or other small instruments, you might like to add them to "O When the Saints Go Marchin' In"; it will be the anthem the children offer to the congregation on Sunday, so making it upbeat and celebratory entirely fits the energy of the day. Print the lyrics in Sunday's bulletin, as the congregation will very much want to join in the fun of singing this hymn!

At the Arts Camp Sunday service, "The Twelve Saints of Arts Camp" will be a part of the collective Offering, while "Make Me a Channel of Your Peace" will be the communion hymn, which Campers will sing to the congregation.

Note: Have those Campers who take communion go first just the way the choir normally would, so you'll have them back to begin singing while communion continues.

We also had a lot of fun in music playing a song game we riffed off the game "We are dancing in the forest." Here are directions:

1. One child is chosen to be *St. George* or *St. Joan*. That child finds a place to "hide,'" but this is not a seeking game so it's more about being outside the rest of the group.

2. Everyone else is a *dragon*. Making dragon faces and motions (but without actually touching each other), they stalk and "fly" about, and chant, "We are dragons playing in the forest, for the saints are far away. Who knows what will happen to us, if they find us at our play?"

3. Then they all stop and cry, "St. George (or St. Joan), are you there?"

4. The *saint* can say "Yes" or "No":
   — If the *saint* says "Yes," then all the *dragons* turn away from the *saint's* hiding place, throw their arms in the air and cry "Aaahhhh!" as if in fear of being caught. The saint tiptoes up behind and taps any dragon, who then becomes the next saint.
   — If the *saint* chooses to say "No," then s/he must also state an activity that prevents her or him from coming to catch the *dragons* at their play. For instance, "No, I'm busy taming a wolf!" If this happens, the *dragons* begin to "play" and chant

again. The second time, the *saint* must say "Yes" and come trade places with a *dragon*.

MOVEMENT/DRAMA

We spend the Drama/Movement sessions of this week hearing stories of additional saints and then using items from a dress-up box to reenact those stories. This is where Campers learned more about St. Francis—specifically the story of Francis taming a wolf. They also heard and role-played the stories of St. Clare, St. Brigid and her cloak, and St. Patrick and his capture and kidnapping, as well as his escape and return.

A stack of storybooks from our own shelves and from the local library were all the resources we needed for this time.

Start, especially on the first day or two, in a circle with a simple song or movement activity before having Campers sit down to hear a story. Pick stories with some action! Also choose those, like St. Brigid's, with a good dose of divine mystery. Read and re-read the stories you've chosen until you can tell them more than reading them, making the telling dramatic and exciting and leaving out any parts you feel detract from the excitement or magic of the story.

Next, have a dress-up box prepared with as wide a variety of items as possible. Scarves and lightweight blankets are great, as are masks if you have appropriate ones and any cloth with a fur-like feel and appearance. You will need a blue cloth for Brigid's cloak, for sure. Pieces of cloth in earth tones are wonderful for quickly creating scenery: blue for water, green for grass or plants, brown for the earth or desert. We even had Campers dress one of our Counselors as a forest, which he played enthusiastically.

Divide the items from the dress-up box into two piles ahead of time, to avoid conflict when it's time to choose.

Have Campers divide into two groups (remember you already have a smaller group from the full camp) and give them a few minutes to decide who plays what or whom, what materials they'll use, and to practice retelling the story once. This is a time when the themes of friendship and working together can become important, as more than one child might be extremely wedded to a particular part.

Usually a reminder that we are all sharing this week, that we're learning the value of giving as well as receiving, is enough to move through. If you end up with two kids in one group who seem to be in constant conflict, make a quick switch with an older child from the other group. We had one child who demanded her own way two days in a row, threatening tears until another child gave in both times. On the third day I kindly but firmly said, "No, you've gotten your first choice two times now, it's her turn to choose." I thought the first child would refuse to participate and was prepared for that, but in the end she reacted rather gracefully and helped her erstwhile foe into the costume she'd just been insisting on wearing herself.

On Thursday, once you've opened your session with a Drama/Movement activity, sit everyone down and ask them what they've learned or heard this week that they'd like to share with the congregation on Sunday (to include in the Offering). Scribe as they go, asking clarifying questions and flushing out completion of ideas. Some children will offer several thoughts, while you will need to encourage others to give you anything at all. We had a very young six-year-old at this camp who couldn't come up with anything, mostly because she enjoyed her own daydreams most of the day. Finally, pushed gently to tell me something she'd learned during camp, she smiled and said glowingly, "God is everywhere!" We couldn't have asked for better.

Between Thursday afternoon and Friday's rehearsal, Adult Volunteers will compile all of the Campers' statements and put them into an order with some flow to it. We like to scribe the Campers' thoughts on index cards to help with this process. Don't be afraid to edit and revise, as long as you keep the Camper's original thought intact. Add a bit, especially to the lines of Campers whom you know to be confident speakers and readers. Even add full, new lines that you feel would enhance the

Offering or are needed for cohesion, and offer them to older Campers.

For Friday's rehearsal, have highlighted "scripts" prepared for each Camper. Ask Campers to line up in order of their parts, and pass a handheld microphone down the line when they present their collective Offering. *Note:* We had a few older Campers who'd come up with several statements that ended up in different places in the Offering for the sake of flow. For these kids, we rehearsed and used two or even three "marks" on the floor; these Campers simply read their first part, passed the mic, and then quietly slipped behind the group to their next mark in time for their second line. This worked fine with kids who were old enough and paying attention, and you'll be pleasantly surprised at how they rise to the occasion, given the opportunity and trust.

Lastly, decide on a place within your offering for the Campers to sing "The Twelve Saints of Arts Camp."

POPSICLES/SNACK, GAMES, AND CLOSING THE CAMP DAY

See Chapter 6 (p. 35) for the specifics of how to end the day and Appendix 3 (p. 117) for a list of tried-and-true camp games.

FRIDAY AFTERNOON

Before you pray and sing, which should be the last act of the last day of Arts Camp, you may want to leave time for an evaluation. A simple evaluation form can be found in Appendix 2 (p. 114).

You'll also want to make sure Campers take home the things they brought with them at the beginning of the week and that have accumulated throughout camp: water bottles, beach towels, sweaters and sweatshirts, hats and sunglasses. Also send home any art projects that you do *not* want to use or display on Sunday. Keep tie-dye shirts and everything else they will wear or display on Sunday.

You'll want your Art Instructor(s) and Counselors to spend time following the last Art session on Friday setting up a display of the Campers' creations so that is in place for Sunday.

Finally, send a note home with each family on Friday afternoon thanking them for bringing their children to camp and giving them details on the Sunday service, including what time Campers should arrive. You want time for Campers to put on their tie-dye shirts and to come to the choir loft to practice before the service begins. A sample of this note home can be found with the forms in Appendix 2 (p. 113). We copy this note on brightly colored paper and place it next to the sign-out sheet for parents to see and take when they come to pick up their Campers.

As with every day of Arts Camp, but especially on Friday, you'll want your Counselors to stay later so they can help you put camp away!

Throughout the week, we have parents who tend to arrive to pick up their children a little early, so they've seen and heard our closing prayer and song. On Friday, once we've given instructions for taking things home and final cleanup, invite parents and caregivers to join the circle at this time. Then try not to get emotional as you sing your goodbye blessing and realize that Arts Camp is over for the year.

PART THREE | Appendices

Appendix 1: Resources

MUSIC

- *The Hymnal 1982,* The Church Hymnal Corporation, New York, NY, 1985

- *Wonder Love and Praise,* Church Publishing Incorporated, New York, NY, 1997

- *Lift Every Voice and Sing II,* The Church Hymnal Corporation, New York, NY, 1993

- *The New Century Hymnal,* The Pilgrim Press, Cleveland, OH, 1995

- *My Heart Sings Out,* Church Publishing Incorporated, New York, NY, 2005

- *Lifesongs*, Augsburg Fortress, Minneapolis, MN, 1999

- *The Tune Book,* Songs and Creations, Inc., San Anselmo, CA, 1982

- http://www.hymnary.org

- http://www.choristersguild.org

- http://www.seasonsonline.ca

- http://www.songsforteaching.com

- http://www.irish-folk-songs.com

- http://www.youtube.com/watch?v=ODftYTD3Rbs

- http://www.youtube.com/watch?v=o-86InqLkYc

- Who Is My Neighbor? Sheet music available below

- http://www.sacredmusicradio.org

- http://www.mtrs.co.uk/rounds.htm

- https://www.youtube.com/watch?v=KRZaop5ZoJA

- https://www.giamusic.com/sacred_music/index.cfm

- https://www.youtube.com/watch?v=EOhZujNbYg8

- http://www.musicnotes.com

- http://www.jan-leemusic.com/Site/History.html

ART MATERIALS

- http://www.raft.net

- https://www.youtube.com/watch?v=MeTh8AjxmPc

- http://www.crazycrow.com

- http://www.worldpeacevillage.org

- http://www.wikihow.com/Draw-a-Mandala

- http://www.dha choristers guild rmashop.com

- http://www.grateful-dyes.com

- http://www.hud.gov/offices/pih/ih/codetalk/planet/connect_medicinewheel.html

LITURGY FOR ARTS CAMP SUNDAY

- http://crucix.com/welsh/communion/cinw-hc-english.pdf

RESOURCES FOR MORNING PROGRAMS

- *The Barefoot Book of Blessings from Many Faiths and Cultures,* Barefoot Books, Cambridge, MA, 1999

- *Spark Story Bible,* Augsburg Fortress, Minneapolis, MN, 2009

- *Children of God Storybook Bible,* Archbishop Desmond Tutu, Zondervan, Grand Rapids, MI, 2010

- http://www.brainyquote.com

- http://www.lectionarypage.net

- http://www.ultimatecampresource.com

- http://www.episcopalrelief.org/church-in-action/christian-formation/christian-formation-for-children – Abundant

- *The Barefoot Book of Earth Tales,* Dawn Casey, Barefoot Books, Cambridge, MA, 2009

- http://www.creatormundi.com/product/the-original-mealtime-prayer-cube

- http://www.users.ms11.net/~gsong/Graces/first-lines/first.html

- *One World, Many Religions,* Mary Pope Osborne, Alfred A. Knopf, New York, NY, 1996

- *The Kids Book of World Religions,* Jennifer Glossop, Kids Can Press, Toronto, ON, 2003

- http://www.stnicholascenter.org

BOOKS AND STORIES

Chapter 7: Praise!

- *Let the Whole Earth Sing Praise,* Tomie dePaola, GP Putnam's Sons Books for Young Readers, New York, NY, 2011

- *Because Nothing Looks Like God,* Lawrence and Karen Kushner, Jewish Lights Publishing, Woodstock, VT, 2000

- *God in Between,* Sandy Eisenberg Sasso, Jewish Lights Publishing, Woodstock, VT, 1998

- *All the World,* Liz Garton Scanlon, Beach Lane Books, New York, NY, 2009

- *Light the Candle! Bang the Drum!,* Ann Morris, Dutton Children's Books, New York, NY, 1997

Chapter 8: EcoJustice

- *God Created,* Mark Bozzuti-Jones, Augsburg Books, Minneapolis, MN, 2003

- *Song of the Water Boatman & Other Pond Poems,* Joyce Sidman, Houghton Mifflin Co., Boston, MA, 2005

- *The Carrot Seed,* Ruth Krauss, HarperCollins, New York, NY, 1973

- *The Mountain that Loved a Bird,* Alice McLerran, Scholastic Inc., New York, NY, 1985

- *Nature's Green Umbrella,* Gail Gibbons, HarperCollins, New York, NY, 1997

- *The Lorax,* Dr. Seuss, Random House, New York, NY, 1971

Chapter 9: Who Is My Neighbor?

- *Me!*, Philip Waechter, Handprint Books, Brooklyn, NY, 2004
- *God in Between*, Sandy Eisenberg Sasso, Jewish Lights Publishing, Woodstock, VT, 1998
- *Yertle the Turtle*, Dr. Seuss, Random House, New York, NY, 1950

Chapter 10: Interfaith Peace

- *Small Acts of Kindness*, James Vollbracht, Paulist Press, Mahwah, NJ, 1995
- *Jesus Goes to School*, Carrie Lou Goddard, Abingdon Press, Nashville, TN, 1999
- *The Legend of the Bluebonnet*, Tomie dePaola, The Putnam & Grosset Group, New York, NY, 1983
- *Giving Thanks*, Chief Jake Swamp, Lee & Low Books Inc., New York, NY, 1995
- *Moody Cow Meditates*, Kerry Lee MacLean, Wisdom Publications, Boston, MA, 2009
- *The Little Book of Hindu Deities*, Sanjay Patel, Plume, New York, NY, 2006
- *A Hindu Creation Story*, https://www.youtube.com/watch?v=Y9yWwFWpbRo

Chapter 11: Saints and Holy Helpers

- *I Sing a Song of the Saints of God*, Lesbia Scott, Morehouse Publishing, New York, NY, 1981
- *Clown of God*, Tomie dePaola, Harcourt Brace, New York, NY, 1978
- *A Saint and His Lion*, Elaine Murray Stone, Paulist Press, Mahwah, NJ, 2004
- *Brigid's Cloak*, Bryce Milligan, Eerdmans Publishing, Grand Rapids, MI, 2002
- *St. George and the Dragon*, Margaret Hodges, Little, Brown, and Company, New York, NY, 1984
- *Peter Claver, Patron Saint of Slaves*, Julia Durango, Paulist Press, Mahwah, NJ, 2002
- *The Monk Who Grew Prayer*, Claire Brandenburg, Ancient Faith Publishing, Chesterton, IN, 2003

THE STORY OF ST. FRANCIS
(A STORY-BOX STORY)

© Kathleen Crevasse 2007. Used with permission.

Note: Tell the story of St. Francis using a story box containing the following items:

- strip of burlap about 12" by 24" to use as an underlay as you tell the story
- statue or picture of St. Francis
- fake gold coins (easily found at craft and party stores)
- wrapped piece of candy
- toy or statue of a soldier or knight
- length of chain (easily purchased at a hardware store)
- piece of rich-looking cloth, like silk or velvet
- small piece of rough cloth, cut in the shape of a robe, and a piece of string for a belt
- sun, a moon, and some stars (stickers, pictures, etc.)
- small animal figures and some rocks
- nativity figures, particularly the Holy Family and stable beasts
- a printed copy of Saint Francis' prayer ("Make me an instrument of your peace...")

Place the story box beside you. Prop the lid up against the box so that the kids can't see what's inside. Unroll the burlap. Say:

This is a story about a man named Francis. Actually, he started out with the name John—or *Giovanni*—which is how you say John in Italy where he was born.

Place the statue of Francis on the burlap. Say:

Francis' father had just returned from France, a country he fell in love with, when the new baby was born. He insisted he be called Francis (*Francesco* in Italian) to honor the place he loved so much.

Place a pile of gold coins on the burlap at your far right. You will place the objects from your right to your left, so that it will read like a book for the children. Say:

Francis was born into a very wealthy family in Assisi, Italy. His father traded fine cloths all over Europe. The family lived very well.

Place a piece of wrapped candy (like a peppermint) on the burlap. Say:

When Francis was a young man, he loved living the good life his wealth allowed. He had a huge fondness for sweets; he loved to go to parties; he was a leader among the young people of Assisi.

Place the knight and then the chain on the burlap. Say:

When Assisi went to war, Francis went off to fight but ended up in prison. He then was sick for a long time. When he was finally well enough to return to fight—in all new clothes and armor—he started to question his path. The way he looked at the world was starting to change.

Pretend to distribute the coins. Say:

Praying to God, drawing so close to God that he knew what God wanted him to do, he started to give away many of his belongings to beggars and lepers. He tried to see what life was like for them.

Place a cross on the burlap. Say:

One day, while praying in a church before the large cross there, he heard a voice come from the cross, saying, "Francis, don't you see that my house is falling down? Go and rebuild it."

Place the cloth on the burlap. Say:

He ran and took a bolt of cloth from his home, sold it and tried to offer money to the priest of the church to help him rebuild it.

From then on, Francis devoted his life more and more to God. His father didn't like this at all. He had Francis brought before a court to try to get him to return to

his old life or give back everything he'd ever received from his father.

Place a robe and belt on burlap (cut rough cloth into robe shape, tie belt with string). Say:

Francis took off every stitch of his clothing and said, "I give everything back to you that you gave me. I now call no one father but God."

Following the gospel call to go out taking no money, not even a walking stick or shoes for the road, Francis gave up his fine clothes and started wearing a simple woven robe made of rough cloth, tied with a rope for a belt. He committed himself to a life of poverty.

As much as Francis rejected money, he loved everything in the created world. He saw God's presence everywhere, in everything.

Put sun, moon, and stars on burlap. Say:

He called the sun his brother, the moon and the stars his sisters, the earth his mother. He was deeply attached to nature.

Place animals and rocks on burlap. Say:

The animals were his family.

Soon other people wanted to live their lives like Francis. They sold all their things and gave their money to the poor. Francis' way of life became a model for a growing group. Soon, they became a religious order, a brotherhood of monks. They would come to be known as the Franciscans. Francis' friend, Clare, formed a group of women, also devoted to a life of poverty.

Place a nativity scene on burlap. Say:

Francis staged the first living crèche scene. He set up a stable with live animals one Christmas to honor Jesus' birth and let people contemplate what it must have been like.

Francis tried to live his life according to what Jesus taught. He took the gospels seriously and tried to live them. He trusted God to take care of his needs. He prayed to be more like Jesus.

Francis finally died as he lived, poor and faithful. The order of Franciscans grew and grew. There are now Franciscan brothers all over the world. We remember Saint Francis for his commitment to the poor, his faithful love of God, and his love for all of creation. And we remember the prayer he gave us.

Read St Francis' Prayer to Campers.

WHO IS MY NEIGHBOR?

Words and Music © Mary Ellen Garrett, Denver, CO. Used with permission.

Note from the composer: I was inspired to write this song for our parish youth after participating in an excellent study and discussion series on immigration by the Colorado Council of Churches: http://www.cochurches.org/publications-curriculums/who-is-my-neighbor/, and by the questions and challenges that come up every day in city life. The song doesn't answer these questions, but I hope it encourages thoughtful and compassionate engagement with them. Please feel free to play around with call and response (different singers taking turns with the lines), add harmonies onto the ending, and accompany with any instruments you and your young singers like: piano, guitar, drums, horns, rock band.

Appendix 2: Sample Forms, Notes Home, and Evaluations

Note: You are free to adapt any of these forms, letters, and lists. Some can be printed and used as is or by adding your own information: 1–5, 7, 9–10. The two letters are provided as samples only: 6 and 8; use these two as models to create your own letters for families.

Camper Registration and Pledge

Arts Camp, sponsored by: _____

Dates of Camp: _____ Registration Deadline: _____

Name of Camper: _____

Age: _____ Current Grade: _____

T-shirt size: adult S M L or youth X S S M L (please circle)

Parent(s) Name(s): _____

1st Phone Contact: _____

2nd Phone Contact: _____

3rd Phone Contact:_____

(Please list phone #s according to priority as emergency contacts, and indicate which parent we should ask for at that number.)

Email(s): _____

Address: _____

Emergency Contact (other than parent/guardian)

Name: _____

Phone(s): _____

Relationship to Camper: _____

Fee for camp is $_____ .

A deposit of $_____ per camper is due with this registration packet, with the remaining $_____ due on _____.

Please make checks payable to: _____

CAMP REGISTRATION CHECKLIST:

_____ Registration Packet (due   )

_____ $___ Deposit (per Junior Counselor, due with Registration)

_____ Consent for Participation and Counselors' Pledge

_____ Medical Information and Authorization Form

Consent for Camp Participation and Campers' Pledge

Event: Arts Camp

Dates and Times: _____

Event Location: _____

PARENTS:

I/We grant permission for _____ (child's name) to participate in Arts Camp.

Arts Camp will take place _____, from _____ to _____, and Campers will share an Offering with the congregation at the _____ service on _____. Campers are to be dropped off no earlier than _____ and picked up by _____ each day.

Camp fees are $_____ per Camper, with a $____ deposit due with this registration packet. The $_____ balance will be due no later than _____. This fee includes lunch and snacks each day of camp and a t-shirt for each Camper, in addition to costs of camp including but not limited to paying for instructors and materials.

Parent or Guardian:_____ Date:_____

PARENTS AND CAMPERS:

We understand that for every Camper to have the most fun, it is important that everyone attending Arts Camp participates fully and with a good spirit. Therefore we agree to the following pledge, as shown by our signatures:

I (the Camper) will participate fully in each activity.

I will show respect for Instructors and Leaders, Counselors, other Campers, myself, and the building and materials around me.

Should there be any misunderstanding between myself and another Camper, I will first try to work it out with that person. If I need help, I will talk to a camp Counselor or Leader.

If I am unable or unwilling to participate in a safe and constructive manner, my parents/guardians and I fully understand that they will be contacted and I will be sent home from camp. Arts Camp will not be able to refund the camp fee if I should be sent home for reasons of non-compliance or disruptive or unsafe behavior.

Camper Signature: _____

Parent/Guardian Signature: _____

Date: _____

Junior Counselor Registration and Pledge

Arts Camp, sponsored by: _____

Dates of Camp: _____Registration Deadline: _____

Name of Camper: _____

Age: _____ Current Grade: _____

T-shirt size: adult S M L or youth X S S M L (please circle)

Parent(s) Name(s): _____

1st Phone Contact: _____

2nd Phone Contact: _____

3rd Phone Contact: _____

(Please list phone #s according to priority as emergency contacts, and indicate which parent we should ask for at that number.)

Email(s): _____

Address: _____

Emergency Contact (other than parent/guardian)

Name: _____

Phone(s): _____

Relationship to Camper: _____

Fee for camp is $_____ .

Fee for Junior Counselors is $_____ to offset cost of food and a t-shirt and is due with this registration packet

Please make checks payable to: _____

CAMP REGISTRATION CHECKLIST:

_____ Registration Packet (due _____)

_____ $_____ Deposit (per Junior Counselor, due with Registration)

_____ Consent for Participation and Counselors' Pledge

_____ Medical Information and Authorization Form

Consent for Camp Participation and Counselors' Pledge

Event: Arts Camp

Dates and Times: _____

Event Location: _____

PARENTS:

I/We grant permission for _____ (child's name)
to participate in Arts Camp.

Arts Camp will take place _____, from _____ to _____, and Campers will share an Offering
with the congregation at the _____ service on _____. Campers are to be dropped off no earlier
than _____ and picked up by _____ each day.

Camp fees are $_____ per Camper, with a $_____ deposit due with this registration packet. The $_____
balance will be due no later than _____. This fee includes lunch and snacks each day of camp and a
t-shirt for each Camper, in addition to costs of camp including but not limited to paying for instructors and materials.

Parent or Guardian: _____ Date: _____

PARENTS AND CAMPERS:

We understand that for every Camper to have the most fun, it is important that everyone attending Arts Camp participates fully and with a good spirit. Therefore we agree to the following pledge, as shown by our signatures:

As a Junior Counselor, I will participate fully in each activity and will be a positive role model for younger Campers.

I will show respect for Instructors and Leaders, other Counselors, Campers, myself, and the building and materials
around me and model that respect for the Campers.

I will strive to act as a mentor and helper to the Campers, but will ask an older Counselor or Adult for help if I need it.

If I am unable or unwilling to model positive and helpful behaviors, my parents/guardians and I fully understand that
they will be contacted and I will be sent home from camp. Arts Camp will not be able to refund the camp fee if I should
be sent home for reasons of non-compliance or disruptive or unsafe behavior.

Junior Counselor Signature: _____

Parent/Guardian Signature: _____

Date: _____

Senior Counselor Registration and Pledge

Arts Camp, sponsored by: _____

Dates of Camp: _____Registration Deadline: _____

Name of Camper: _____

Age: _____ Current Grade: _____

T-shirt size: adult S   M   L   or youth X S   S   M   L   (please circle)

Parent(s) Name(s): _____

1st Phone Contact: _____

2nd Phone Contact: _____

3rd Phone Contact: _____

(Please list phone #s according to priority as emergency contacts, and indicate which parent we should ask for at that number.)

Email(s): _____

Address: _____

Emergency Contact (other than parent/guardian)

Name: _____

Phone(s): _____

Relationship to Camper: _____

Fee for camp is $_____ .

Fee for Senior Counselors is $_____ to offset cost of food and a t-shirt and is due with this registration packet

Please make checks payable to: _____

CAMP REGISTRATION CHECKLIST:

_____ Registration Packet (due_____)

_____ $_____ Deposit (per Senior Counselor, due with Registration)

_____ Consent for Participation and Counselors' Pledge

_____ Medical Information and Authorization Form

Consent for Camp Participation and Counselors' Pledge

Event: Arts Camp

Dates and Times: _____

Event Location: _____

PARENTS:

I/We grant permission for _____ (*youth's name*) to participate in Arts Camp.

Arts Camp will take place _____, from _____ to _____, and Campers and Senior Counselors will share an Offering with the congregation at the _____ service on _____. Campers are to be dropped off no earlier than _____ and picked up by _____ each day.

Camp fees are $____ per Senior Counselor, due with this registration packet. This fee includes lunch and snacks each day of camp and a T-shirt for each Senior Counselor.

Parent or Guardian:_____ Date:_____

PARENTS AND CAMPERS:

We understand that for every Camper to have the most fun, it is important that everyone attending Arts Camp participates fully and with a good spirit. Therefore we agree to the following pledge, as shown by our signatures:

As a Senior Counselor, I will take on a leadership role in helping Campers to follow directions, to participate in and complete activities, and to problem solve when needed.

I will show respect for Instructors and Leaders, other Counselors, Campers, myself, and the building and materials around me, and will model that respect for the Campers.

I will strive to act as a mentor and helper to both the Campers and the Junior Counselors.

I understand that I am not signing up to attend Arts Camp as a Camper. When possible, I will be able to participate in projects, but my main role will be to help the camp run smoothly and safely. I further understand that if I choose not to fulfill my duties, my parents/guardian will be called to take me home and camp fees will not be refunded.

Senior Counselor Signature: _____

Parent/Guardian Signature: _____

Date: _____

Medical Release

Medical Information and Authorization

Event: Arts Camp

Dates and Times: _____

Event Location: _____

Participant's Name: _____ Birth Date: _____

Medical Information: _____

_____

_____

_____

Doctor's Name and Phone Number: _____

_____

Health Information and Medications: _____

_____

_____

_____

_____

Allergies (please include ALL known allergies, including food and medication): ___

_____

_____

_____

_____

Special Needs/Other important information about my child: _____

_____

_____

_____

_____

_____

Medical Release

Insurance Information: _____

_____

_____

_____

I/We have medical insurance coverage for the above named participant. _____

Company: _____

_____

_____

_____

Policy #: _____

Address: _____

Name of Policy Holder: _____

Group #: _____

○ I/We acknowledge that the above named participant is not covered by any medical insurance policy and understand that I/we are responsible for all costs.

In the event of an emergency, I understand that *every* effort will be made to contact me as quickly as possible. I hereby authorize an adult leader of this activity to act as agent for me to consent to any medical, dental, or surgical treatment necessary by a licensed medical professional. I acknowledge that I am financially responsible for any emergency medical or dental costs.

Parent/Guardian Name (please print): _____

Signature: _____ Date: _____

Photo Waiver

I, _____, the parent or legal guardian of

(print adult's name)

(Camper's & Counselor's name[s] . . . *please list all from your family!*)

_____

_____

_____

_____

_____

give permission to use my child[ren]'s image in the following formats:

| Yes | No | In-house displays of Arts Camp |

Yes   No   In-house displays of Arts Camp

Yes   No   On the _____ public website

Yes   No   Future Arts Camp flyers

Yes   No   The _____ Facebook page

Children's names will never be posted with their photos on any of the above formats.

Please don't hesitate to be specific; we fully understand that while some families aren't worried about their children's photos being "out there" for others, it is a serious concern and possible safety issue. We will honor your requests to the letter and always err on the side of caution if we are in any doubt.

Sample: Letter Home

(1 WEEK BEFORE ARTS CAMP BEGINS)

Dear Arts Camp Parents,

Thank you for bringing your child to St. Barnabas' annual summer Arts Camp. We are planning a wonderful week of friendship, art, music, drama, and games.

Your child should bring a yoga mat or beach towel and a water bottle to camp every day, all marked with her/his name. The bottle can go home and be refilled daily or we can refill it here at the church and place it in the refrigerator after camp each day.

Note that, in addition to the Monday–Friday, 9:00 a.m.–3:00 p.m. camp days, we do expect Campers—and of course invite their families—to join our 9:30 a.m. service on Sunday, June 22, to share what we've discovered about the saints as helpers and peacemakers. It is very hard for Campers to prepare all week and then miss Sunday's celebration, so please plan to be here. *Campers need to be at church by 8:45 a.m. Sunday.* Thanks!

We are going on a field trip!

Thursday morning we will meet at our community garden plots located at Colfax and Josephine. At the garden we will sing, play, plant and harvest while we focus on how sustainable farming and eating relates to loving our neighbors.

Every Camper should come Thursday morning with a good sun hat and sunscreen already applied.

PLEASE DROP YOUR CHILD OFF AT THE EAST HIGH SCHOOL ESPLANADE (across Colfax from the Tattered Cover). I will have the sign-in sheet with us, so please bring your child to me. We will walk together back to St. Barnabas at 10:00 a.m..

Please sign below to indicate that you give permission for your child to be on this walking field trip with us, and return the bottom portion as soon as possible:

I _____ (parent's name) give permission for my child,

_____ (child's name) to join with St. Barnabas' Arts Camp leaders at the

community garden at Colfax and Josephine and to walk with the leaders back to the church.

------------------------------   ------------------

(Parent signature)   (date)

Arts Camp Sign-In/Sign-Out

Parents/Caregivers: Please initial both when you drop your child(ren) off in the morning and when you pick them up in the afternoon. Thanks!

NAME	MON AM	MON PM	TUE AM	TUE PM	WED AM	WED PM	THU AM	THU PM	FRI AM	FRI PM

Sample: Friday Note Home Regarding Arts Camp Sunday

ARTS CAMP WORSHIP THIS SUNDAY . . .

Who: ALL CAMPERS and COUNSELORS

What: "The Saints of God" Presentation to our families/friends at St. Barnabas

When: THIS SUNDAY, JUNE 22 8:45 a.m. rehearsal/warm up, 9:30 a.m. service, treats to follow

Where: St. Barnabas Episcopal Church, 13th & Vine St.

Why: Because we've spent an amazing week together, and now it's time to share what we've made and learned!!

PLEASE PLAN TO BE THERE WITH YOUR FAMILY

- -

ARTS CAMP WORSHIP THIS SUNDAY . . .

Who: ALL CAMPERS and COUNSELORS

What: "The Saints of God" Presentation to our families/friends at St. Barnabas

When: THIS SUNDAY, JUNE 22 8:45 a.m. rehearsal/warm up, 9:30 a.m. service, treats to follow

Where: St. Barnabas Episcopal Church, 13th & Vine St.

Why: Because we've spent an amazing week together, and now it's time to share what we've made and learned!!

PLEASE PLAN TO BE THERE WITH YOUR FAMILY

- -

ARTS CAMP WORSHIP THIS SUNDAY . . .

Who: ALL CAMPERS and COUNSELORS

What: "The Saints of God" Presentation to our families/friends at St. Barnabas

When: THIS SUNDAY, JUNE 22 8:45 a.m. rehearsal/warm up, 9:30 a.m. service, treats to follow

Where: St. Barnabas Episcopal Church, 13th & Vine St.

Why: Because we've spent an amazing week together, and now it's time to share what we've made and learned!!

PLEASE PLAN TO BE THERE WITH YOUR FAMILY

Evaluation Form

What did you like at this Arts Camp? _____

_____

What new ideas did you learn or explore? _____

_____

What would you improve about Arts Camp? _____

_____

Would you recommend this Arts Camp to a friend?   Yes   No

Would you like to come back next year?   Yes   No

Would you like to be a Junior or Senior Counselor
when you're old enough?   Yes   No

	Liked a lot	OK	Didn't Like
MORNING GATHERING	1	2	3
ART	1	2	3
MUSIC	1	2	3
MOVEMENT/DRAMA	1	2	3
STORIES	1	2	3
GAMES	1	2	3
LUNCH	1	2	3

What else would you like us to know about your Arts Camp experience? _____

_____

_____

_____

_____

Lunch Setup and Cleanup for Volunteers

SETUP

- [ ] Wash 1 head of lettuce, 2 tomatoes, 1 container grapes (On Tuesday–Thursday please check for leftovers first.)

- [ ] Set up 2 long tables for buffet-style lunch.

- [ ] Set out plates (yellow and blue plastic) and napkins.

- [ ] Put 1 container each of turkey and ham, about 25 slices of cheese, and lettuce and tomatoes on platters.

- [ ] Put mayo and mustard on buffet table with about 4 butter knives.

- [ ] Keep peanut butter and jelly in kitchen, but ready with knives.

- [ ] Fill bowl with carrots and snap peas, put out with tongs.

- [ ] Fill bowl with 1 bag chips, put out with tongs.

- [ ] Choose and set out 1 variety of dessert for 30 people.

- [ ] Set out cups and lemonade cooler at far end of table, with drip catcher underneath to protect carpet; 1 large trash can, 1 recycle bin, 1 bin soapy water w/ sponge, 1 bin rinse water, 1 empty bin—all go outside on grass just left of front door.

CLEANUP

- [ ] Campers will wash and rinse their plates and cups and leave them in the empty bin.

- [ ] Wrap unused food and place in fridge for tomorrow.

- [ ] Wash platters, bowls, and utensils as needed and leave to dry in drainer.

- [ ] Wipe down and put away tables.

- [ ] Empty wash and rinse bins in garden (the soap is biodegradable); bring in trash, recycle bin, and bins and leave them to dry.

THANK YOU FOR BEING HERE TODAY!!

Arts Camp Sunday Program Image

SAINT BARNABAS
ARTS CAMP 2013

St. Barnabas Arts Campers
Wish to Welcome all of You,
our Families and Friends

Arts Campers:
Name all
Campers
here... double
check spellings
to make sure
everyone's name
is listed correctly!

Jr. Counselors
Name all of
your Junior Counselors
and thank them for
their mentorship of
the Campers

MANY THANKS to all those who helped make
this year's Arts Camp not only possible but
incredibly successful......

Senior Counselors

Guest Artists
This is where you name
Your Art Instructors

Thanks also to:
Adult Volunteers,
Lunch Volunteers,
Parish Administrator & Clergy
Parents who helped out, and
Anyone else you haven't already named

Live in Peace and Love

*Out beyond ideas of wrongdoing
and rightdoing there is a field...
I'll meet you there.*

~Rumi

Appendix 3: Games

KIDS' GARDEN

Kids' Garden is a boxed set of forty activities and games, some indoor and some outdoor. We used several of them during our EcoJustice Arts Camp. Look for:

- *Kids' Garden,* Whitney Cohen, Barefoot Books, Cambridge, MA, 2010

ABUNDANT LIFE GARDEN PROJECT

The *Abundant Life Garden Project,* written by Cynthia Coe for The Episcopal Church, has great games, many of which we used at Arts Camp: EcoJustice. Go to:

- https://www.episcopalrelief.org/church-in-action/christian-formation/christian-formation-for-children#Abundant.

MAGIC CARPET

Materials:
- 1 blanket, opened sleeping bag, or tarp for every 5–8 Campers

Directions:
- Ask Campers to remove their shoes (socks are optional).
- Divide Campers into teams of 5–8. Each team should be able to stand on its "magic carpet" without touching each other. *Note:* Depending on Camp dynamics, it's often best to create teams with diversity rather than letting Campers form their own groups. Two quick ways to do this are to have Campers count off while standing in a circle . . . then all the "1s" are on a team, all the "2s," etc. Or, divide them by age groups; it's always fun when the younger kids beat the older kids. The Counselors could be their own team on this one, too.
- Each Camper sits on their tarp or blanket and you tell them that this is their magic carpet. They've flown a thousand feet high into the sky but the magic is wearing off and soon they'll be plummeting to the earth. Their only hope is to turn the magic carpet over; the magic is still powerful on the other side. Because they are a thousand feet up, they certainly can't just step off the carpet to flip it over. So they have to work together to get it done without anyone falling off.
- To extend this activity, once they've done it the first time you can add challenges such as: try using only your feet or try doing it without talking (my favorite!).

FOUR-FOOT WALL (OR SIX-FOOT, OR TEN-FOOT... WHATEVER FITS!)

Materials:

- Blue painters tape or masking tape, or a line of thin rope

Directions:

- Attach your tape or rope at the desired height, to simulate a "wall." It could be as long as your room or only the distance between two trees or cupboard handles (handy for tying rope if they're at the right height). We used 4' because that was challenging for our Campers but still very safe. I also had Senior Counselors "spotting" Campers anytime anyone was being lifted.

- All Campers start on one side of the wall. Their job is to figure out how to get everyone over the wall safely. Whether they can use objects such as chairs and stools is up to you. Obviously, it's more challenging without, but safety should always take priority, even over team building!

BACK TO BACK

Materials:

- Campers!

Directions:

- Invite Campers to form pairs. It's better if partners are similar in height, but more challenging if they're not.
- Each pair sits on the floor, back to back.
- Without using their hands, each pair attempts to stand up. The pressure and balance of leaning into each other's backs is what makes this work. If one person in the pair pops up alone, then they have not completed the task; ask them to try again.

- Once they've done this (usually quite quickly), have them try it in groups of three and then four, which requires much more communication and teamwork.

- *Fun variation:* Put everyone in a large circle, facing sideways, so everyone has his/her back touching one neighbor and is facing his/her other neighbor. Then see if the entire group can stand at the same exact moment by pushing against backs while simultaneously holding the hands of the person in front of them.

CRISS-CROSS BALL

Materials:

- 2 lengths of rope, long enough to stretch across the room
- 4 chairs or other furniture on which to tie the ropes
- 4 soft balls (foam or inflatable) or inflated balloons

Directions:

- Attach the ropes to the chairs diagonally, so they cross in the middle of your space. This should create an X shape, with four spaces between the ropes.
- Divide Campers into four teams.
- Each team *sits* in one of the sections of the X. During the game, everyone must stay seated (not kneeling). Campers should have space to reach both arms out and around them without hitting another camper.

- You will toss the ball/balloon into the X and each team must keep it from hitting the floor. If a Camper gets off his/her seat once, give a warning. The second time that Camper is out.

- As they get comfortable, throw another ball or balloon into the game. Now they must keep both off the floor.

- IF you want to keep score, position Senior Counselors at each of the 4 sections. They keep track of the times the team in front of them let the ball or balloon fall to the floor.

ENDANGERED-SPECIES WALK

Materials:

- a list of printed pictures of endangered species, easily found (*In a pinch, write the names of endangered animals on sheets of paper.*)
- music player, for example, an MP3 player and docking station, CD player, etc.
- recorded music (*The best choice for this game would be a recording of "Whole World."*)

Directions:

- This is a variation of Musical Chairs, which we used for our EcoJustice Arts Camp.
- Lay the photos or written names of endangered animals on the floor in a large circle. You need one per Camper to start with.
- Each Camper stands at the place of one animal.
- Start the music, and have Campers walk from animal to animal around the circle while the music plays.
- Have a Counselor remove one species from the circle.
- Stop the music and have Campers find and stand by one animal. There will be one less spot than there are Campers.
- The Camper who is "out" represents the animal that was removed. Stop to talk about what it would be like if this animal is gone forever. Have that Camper hold the sign representing that animal, on the outside of the circle, while the game continues.
- Clearly, this is a game with a fairly heavy message. Keep it fun; don't dwell too heavily on every single species as it's removed from the circle, but after the game, have Campers look around at all the children and species that are "gone." There should be one Camper and one species left—what would the world be like if that was all that was left? You could intentionally leave a great predator for the last animal; that predator would then have no choice but to eat humans. Or leave something like a bird; but if a bird was the only animal left, what would happen? (It wouldn't have enough food and would quickly become extinct as well.)

RECYCLED OBSTACLE COURSE/OBSTACLE COURSE

Materials:

- large discarded items like boxes, empty tubs, etc. (*The wider your variety, the better. You can also play this game with items you find around the church or home: chairs, hula-hoops, tricycles, etc. We played with our EcoJustice Arts Camp and used items that the Campers then used for their art projects.*)
- creative Counselors

Directions:

- Give 2–3 Senior Counselors extra time beforehand to build an obstacle course using the items you specify. You might want to remind them that the course needs to be fun but safe for all Campers.
- Once they've set it up, have them demonstrate the entire course for the Campers.
- Divide Campers into relay teams; each team sends one player at a time through the course, who then tags the next player to go, and so on. Encourage teamwork and cheering, with a low emphasis on winning. In fact, sometimes our winning team ends up being the group that cheered the loudest or best or most consistently. Once it was the team that cheered for everyone on the course, not just its own teammate.

RECYCLED MINIATURE GOLF

Materials:

- empty jars and cans, with one end completely opened (not like a soda can)
- plastic golf balls, small colorful rubber balls, or small foam balls
- other items to serve as obstacles
- plastic golf clubs or hockey sticks, or large-diameter straws (see *Variation*, below)

Directions:

- This is another time to use your creative Counselors.

Their job is to set up a miniature golf course using the items you've set aside. The open-ended empty cans or jars, lying on their sides, are the holes.

- Once they've set it up, have them take teams of four Campers through to play. If you can have one stick to share per team, all the teams can be playing within a short period of time instead of having kids waiting with nothing to do.
- *Variation:* Set up the course so that kids must get the ball to the hole by blowing on it through a straw.

SAME AND DIFFERENT

This is a good game for getting to know each other at the beginning of an Arts Camp week.

Materials:

- Campers!
- a prepared list of identifying sentences like the following:
  I have 10 toes.
  I love dogs.
  I have an older sister.
  I know how to ski.
  I can skip.
  I am tall for my age.
  I like vegetables.
  I like candy.
  I wish I were older.
  I love school.
  I can swim.
  I love to read.
  I've been to Disneyland.
  I can roller skate.
  I am loved.
  I love my family.
  I love God.
  God loves me!

Directions:

- Have all Campers, Adults, and Counselors sit together in one large circle (adults may want chairs if sitting on the floor is a trial).
- Instructions are simple: "I am going to say a sentence. If the sentence is true for you, stand up. If the sentence is not true for you, sit down."
- Go through the identifying sentences, adding to them or adapting them as best fits your camp. It's fun to single out a special quality a child has if you know about it, such as "I just ran my first 5K race" or "My mom flies planes."

WHO ARE WE?

Materials:

- Campers!
- a list of identifying statements, for example, *I have a cat. I have more than three siblings. I am going into third grade. (You want to have fewer than half your total number of Campers for whom the identifying statement is true.)*

Directions:

- Start with everyone sitting together. Tell Campers: "Stand up and spread out if what I say is true for you." Read one of the identifying statements.
- Remaining Campers then stand up. Each of the Campers in this second group picks a Camper from the first group to approach and talk to, learning her/his name *plus* one other thing about her/him, for example, *What's your cat's name? What school do you go to?*
- Then reassemble and sit back down. Each Camper from the second group introduces the person s/he met: *This is Tim, and his cat's name is Romeo.*
- If you have a group of Campers who mostly know each other well, you might challenge them to try and tell something about themselves that their friends do not already know.
- *Variation:* Give Campers a page with boxes, in each of which is written an identifying statement. Campers then move around the room, finding those for whom each statement is true and writing those names in the boxes. We prefer the paperless game, which emphasizes meeting and talking to each.

SUMMER STORM

Materials:

- Campers!

Directions:

- Sit together in a large circle.
- Explain that the group is going to create a summer storm using nothing but your bodies. Everyone is to copy the move you make, but *not* until the person to the left (or right, it doesn't matter) copies the move first. So you will start, then the Camper to your left will copy, then the next Camper to the left, and so on.
- Start by rubbing your open palms together in a circular motion, which will make a sort of "shushing" sound. Keep doing this until the move has been copied all the way around the circle.
- Next clap your flat hands together lightly. You're not going for the sound of applause, but more of a pat-a-pat noise. Keep going until this sound has gone all the way around the circle. You'll notice that the collective sound builds from something like a light rainfall to heavier rain.
- Switch to snapping your fingers, alternating quickly from hand to hand. Not all the kids will be able to snap, but it's good for them to try, and the sound will increase regardless to something like a heavy rain with possible hail.
- Once the entire circle is snapping, the next move is to slap your hands on the floor, again alternating between hands quickly.
- Now you will reverse the moves, continuing to let each move progress through the whole circle before moving to the next. Your heavy rainstorm will gradually decrease back to a light drizzle.

SILENT BALL

This is a great game for when kids need to move and adults need to bring the noise level down.

Materials:

- soft ball, about the size of a basketball (An inflatable ball also works, but soft is best.)
- space for Campers to spread out enough so that no one can touch anyone else

Directions:

- Explain to Campers that they have until the count of 10 to find a space where they can touch no one and no one can touch them.
- Count slowly, pacing yourself so you get to 10 about the same time as most kids have found a space.
- Explain that once you being playing the game, there is to be silence—no talking, no laughing out loud, no noises. Anyone who talks or makes a noise is out and sits down. (Someone will inevitably ask about sneezing. Tell them that of course sneezing doesn't count if it's real, and that you can *always* tell the difference between a real and a fake sneeze.) The Camp Director or Adult Volunteer leading the game is always allowed to talk, but should refrain from doing so unless absolutely necessary. (I usually ask Senior Counselors to either play with other Campers or work on something in another room; if they're sitting by watching, they will inevitably chat with each other.)

- Simply throwing the ball to each other plays the game. If the throw is good and could be caught, but the catcher drops or misses it, then the catcher is out. If the throw was too high, too low, or too far away and the catcher misses it, then the thrower is out. Once someone is out—for missing a catch, throwing poorly, or talking/noise—s/he sits down right in place and must continue to be silent.
- Once there are only a few Campers left in the game, they must throw more quickly.

UNIVERSAL MUSICAL CHAIRS

This is a physically challenging game with safety considerations and may not be appropriate for every Arts Camp. I inherited this game along with Arts Camp and was reluctant to continue it, as I tend to be over-cautious. Looking back, I deeply appreciate the benefits of facing physical challenge as a group and overcoming struggle through teamwork. Playing Universal Musical Chairs builds trust and community among children and youth and leaves them with a wonderful sense of accomplishment.

We always save this game for the last day of Arts Camp so we can assess the camp community and whether we feel they will be able to play this game safely. That said, this is a perennial favorite for our Campers and Counselors, and it is a joy to watch the older kids lead the younger ones in succeeding at this challenge.

To begin with, you might try dividing into groups of about 8–12 Campers and setting up several smaller versions of this game. Let kids divide into groups that are friendly and work well together. Fewer kids per group will lead to better teamwork and listening, and will give you a chance to become familiar with the way this game works.

No one may wear flip-flops or sandals. Either everyone wears shoes *that stay on* or everyone should be barefoot. Socks are also a bad idea.

Materials:

- solid, non-folding chairs, 1 per camper (We use heavy wooden chairs.)
- Counselors who are responsible, attentive, and good leaders
- music player, like an MP3 player and docking station, CD player, etc.

- recorded music
- a hearty constitution!

Directions:

- Ask Counselors to set up chairs in two rows, set back-to-back, with a single chair facing outward at both ends. Do *not* attempt this game without solid, heavy, non-folding chairs. Set up as many chairs as there are players.
- This is essentially the same as regular Musical Chairs, except no one is ever out and the pace of the game should *not* be frantic but *calm, controlled, and conducive to teamwork.* The idea is that the Campers must fit everyone onto the chairs that are still in the game. There is *no* time limit for doing so.
- When the music begins, Campers start walking around the bank of chairs. One Counselor removes one chair and rearranges the remaining chairs so there are no gaps. Remind that person to be careful of the Campers walking around them as they do this.
- When the music stops, everyone works together to find a way to fit all the Campers on the remaining chairs. *No hands or feet may touch the floor.* Counselors should be spotting at all times to prevent falls, tipping chairs, and other dangers.
- Obviously, this is easy at the beginning and then becomes increasingly difficult as more chairs are removed. Here are some tips we've learned over the years . . . but try to give your Campers and Counselors time to discover them together; you might offer hints and guided questions to help them see new possibilities:
- You can easily fit two Campers to a chair if one is standing and the other is sitting.
- A small Camper can easily perch on a bigger Camper's lap.
- Holding a smaller Camper any other way—for

instance "piggyback"-style or as a parent holds a child on a hip—is against the rules.

- Campers can hold arms or hands to help each other balance.
- If there are support pieces under the seats of the chairs, Campers can slide onto those. Our Counselors wait until everyone seems to be in place, then get down to check for hands or feet on the floor, and if there are none they count "1 . . . 2 . . . 3!" to indicate success.
- Climbing back down to the floor for the next round is when small injuries occur. Campers must take their time, work together, and listen to the Counselors to do this safely.
- The Camp Director *always* reserves the right to "call" the game a win before getting down to one chair. With 24–30 Campers, we generally stop with a sigh of relief at three to four chairs, although one year we made it down to two chairs with about 15 Campers!

This game is absolutely about teamwork. Keep the pacing slow and deliberate. Getting everyone onto the remaining chairs takes thought and communication. Getting them back down to the floor afterwards requires care!

Our Counselors do a great job of leading and also spotting the Campers as they play. They give guidance and help Campers work together to find ways to succeed.

Once no one is touching the floor, the Counselors assist the Campers in climbing down safely. It's important to have everyone watch for fingers and toes, and no one should be jumping from their perch!

One or two Campers usually opt out of this game at some point. They should never be required to play if they don't want to, but can help give advice and ideas with the Counselors.

FIND MORE GAMES HERE

- http://www.ultimatecampresource.com